Bears with an Attitude

Promotional Advocate Toys

Joyce Gerardi Rinehart

Schiffer Publishing Ltd

4880 Lower Valley Road, Atglen, PA 19310 USA

Dedication

This volume is dedicated with love
to my mother, Viola Burton Bryant (1906-1989);
my daughters-in-law Kelly Lee Catto Gerardi,
Maryam Aharinejad Gerardi, Connie Goulet Rinehart,
Carrie Sowers Rinehart and my step-daughters
Dianne Rinehart Houser and Alla Albertovna Rinehart

Note: The name and character of Smokey Bear are the property of the United States Department of Agriculture Forest Service. A portion of the funds realized from the original sale of the Smokey Bear products pictured herein was returned to the Forest Service for the Cooperative Forest Fire Prevention Program. The USDA Forest Service did not authorize this book nor furnish or approve of any of the information contained herein.

This book is not sponsored, authorized, or otherwise affiliated with any of the manufacturers or other companies, agencies, or institutions whose products or logos are featured in this book. The book is derived from the author's independent research.

Diligence has been taken to assure the accuracy of all information and prices presented herein. However, the current values in this book should be used as a guide only. They are not intended to set prices, which fluctuate from one section of the country to another. Auction prices, dealer prices, and flea market and garage sale prices vary greatly and are affected by condition as well as demand. Items in MIB (mint in box), MIP (mint in package), NRFB (never removed from box) condition, or with pristine, all-original clothing, accessories, and tags generally fetch higher prices than those in "played with" condition. Neither the author nor the publisher assumes any responsibility for losses that might be incurred as a result of consulting this guide.

Library of Congress Catalog Card Number: 99-67633

Book Design by Anne Davidsen
Type set in Impress BT/Humanist 521 BT

ISBN: 0-7643-1046-1
Printed in China
1 2 3 4

Published by Schiffer Publishing Ltd.
4880 Lower Valley Road
Atglen, PA 19310
Phone: (610) 593-1777; Fax: (610) 593-2002
E-mail: Schifferbk@aol.com
Please visit our web site catalog at
www.schifferbooks.com

This book may be purchased from the publisher.
Include $3.95 for shipping.
Please try your bookstore first.
We are interested in hearing from authors
with book ideas on related subjects.
You may write for a free catalog.

In Europe, Schiffer books are distributed by
Bushwood Books
6 Marksbury Ave.
Kew Gardens
Surrey TW9 4JF England
Phone: 44 (0) 208 392-8585; Fax: 44 (0) 208 392-9876
E-mail: Bushwd@aol.com
Free postage in the U.K., Europe; air mail at cost.
Try your bookstore first

Contents

Preface

This book is a "Siamese twin," separated at birth from *The Bear Made Me Buy It: Product Advertising Bears*, when it was determined there was too much material for a single volume, and there was a logical dividing point. While *The Bear Made Me Buy It* covered product advertising bears, *Bears with an Attitude* brings you storybook spokesbears, such as Smokey, Yogi, Paddington, Pooh, the Berenstains, Baloo, and the Care Bears, as well as baseball and other sports team bears; domestic and foreign tourist bears, and bears that get the word out on educational, charitable, and medical products or entities.

Acknowledgments

Although a book bears a single author's name, it is the product of hundreds of contributions from dozens of other people. I'd like to gratefully thank these special people:

Nancy Schiffer, knowledgeable editor and efficient "book surgeon;"

Peter Schiffer, for wine, honey, and publishing me again;

Fire Captain **Richard C. Yokley**, who wrote the sections on Smokey Plush Bears, Hand Puppets, Inflatables, and Advertising Smokey, for generously sharing the results of two decades of research, and for proofreading;

The late **Harry Rossoll**, outstanding artist-illustrator-muralist, for photos and information regarding his "Tree Bear," and for his decades of delightful artwork and "Smokey Says" cartoons,

Jim Van Meter, retired Fire Captain, specialist in fire prevention education for the California Department of Forestry, Smokey collector, founder of "Hot Foot Teddy" Collectors Association, and editor of "Hot Foot Teddy News," for his information and encouragement;

Ginny Kreitler, member of UFDC and the Greater St. Louis Doll Club, for contributing a whole slide program of advertising bears;

Linda Mullins, author and a sweet and savvy lady, for her encouragement;

The late **Jean Laughery** for sharing information and photos of dozens of her advertising bears;

Nancy Vanselow for bears, encouragement, and a museum trip;

Cousin **Joan England Burton**, for our annual junkin' jaunts and successful bear hunts in Indiana;

My youngest son **Greg Gerardi**, who planted the bear collecting seed in our family over thirty years ago, and my eldest son **Mark Gerardi**, who loved Yogi Bear and BooBoo.

Beary best wishes, multitudes of thanks, and bear hugs to these sharing, caring bear collectors who kindly sent me photos, allowed me to photograph their charming advertising bears, or supplied needed information:

Oneida Callaway, Judy and Stewart Callaway, Fredye Cochran, author Kerra Davis, photographer Mary Ann Callaway Dennis, L. Victor Desguin, forest ranger John and Shelley DeWitt, Dee Domroe of the Doll Room, Nancyann Eckhart, Greg Joseph Gerardi, Kelly Lee Catto Gerardi, Maryam A. Gerardi, photographer Vivian L. Gery, Nancy Harmon, Linda Hildebrant, author/columnist Dee Hockenberry, Golden Spur recipient author Ms. Lee Hoffman, Dr. Muriel Hoffman, Jeanne Kalis and Shriner Jim "Yogi" Kalis, Cerissa Katyryniuk, photographer Shane Keating, Nancy Kraus of the award winning Yogi Bear's Jellystone Park Campground in Arcadia, Florida; photographer Robert C. McDonald, Sr., artist/author Kathy Melsheimer, Clark and Sandy McKenzie, Margaret "Peggy" Monahan, Lavonne Morrell, Robert Reed of Antique & Collectible News Service, Robin's Collectibles, Shirley Taylor, Bonnie and Larry Vaughan of Raggedy's and Teddy's, Tom and Joni Gruelle Wannamaker of the Johnny Gruelle Raggedy Ann and Andy Museum in Arcola, Illinois, Canadian writer Jacqueline Wilson, and photographer Russ Wilson.

Kudos to everyone at Ritz Camera for giving me such great service processing more than one hundred rolls of film and thus bringing the bears to colorful life.

Sincere thanks to these individuals, corporations and agencies for their pleasant and helpful assistance: Sherri Zucker of Lee County (Florida) Medical Alliance and Gary Ulik and Elaine Kizewski of the Center for Injury Protection for use of Buckle Bear®; Leisure Systems Inc. on behalf of Hanna-Barbera® for use of Yogi Bear's image, Robert Dagley of the Orvis Company, Jennifer Glomb of the Virginia State Police Association, Dawna Fazio and Michael Kruckenberg of Woodland Enterprises, and George B. Black, Jr. of Teddy Bear Museum of Naples, Florida.

For their help in promotion matters, since the first book, I award salvos and salutes to Richard Cilento for all his hours, efforts, and encouragement. With thanks , too, to Kathy Freda of United Seal & Tag Label Corp, and Cindy and Roland Long of C & R Graphics.

Bear hugs and thanks, as always, to my strong support system: my sons and daughters-in-law who cheer me on, my husband Al who suffers through every mini-crisis with me, co-workers, childhood friends who thankfully are still in my life, friends from several doll clubs and the Tuesday Writers Group. *Muchas gracias*, one and all.

Introduction

Bear Brakes bear painted on auto repair shop in Gold Beach, Oregon, 1994.

Whether drawn on cave walls by proud pre-historic hunters, incised on old British pub signs, or printed on pamphlets and cards, advertising bears of one kind or another have been with us for centuries. Cuddly stuffed Teddy bears (named for President Theodore Roosevelt) appeared on the American scene in 1902, and interest in them has never waned. While campaigning for election in 1904, for publicity purposes, President Teddy stood on the observation platform at the back of the train and tossed teddy bears into the crowds of well-wishers. By 1907 "teddy bear" had become a dictionary entry. Bear collectors, bear artists and manufacturers have increased dramatically in incredible numbers since the late 1970s and early 1980s. A Great Depression campaign promise was "a chicken in every pot." The Hugging Bear Inn of Chester, Vermont now promises guests "a bear in every bed."

Bears advertising products date at least to 1890, yet are not nearly as well known as other types of bears, and for decades were afforded little attention and literally no research. Now, a century later, prestigious bear manufacturers are including advertising bears in their collections and catalogs. Quality and interest have risen, and advertising bears are being scooped up by even the most discriminating collectors. Steiff recently issued a Coca Cola polar bear in a limited edition of 10,000 at $375 each. It seems the days of mailing in $1 and one box top to obtain an advertising item are long gone.

While bears touting products have been manufactured for over a century, bears calling attention to causes: safe driving, beach safety, environmental concerns, seat belt and child protection devices; charitable organizations, educational efforts, and medical products and programs are newer entrants. Make yourself "bear aware" and you will soon notice bears everywhere, getting out the message of numerous organizations. And, adding charming, affordable examples to your bear collection.

Chapter 1

Smokey Bear, Advertising's Senior Statesman

A Half-Century and Still Going Strong

The USDA Forest Service's famous spokesbear works for the government, has his own postage stamp and zip code — and has become quite a collectible. Even small children remember his motto, "Only YOU can prevent forest fires." Over the decades Smokey has starred in songs, comics, story and coloring books, in radio, magazine, newspaper, and TV ads, as well as posters. Pro ball players and movie stars, like Hopalong Cassidy, have posed with him and done public service announcements for him. He has appeared at football and baseball games and in elementary school classrooms, and traveled as far away as Canada and Japan to share his forest safety message. In 1964 Smokey was appointed an honorary member of the Civil Air Patrol, and was given his own personal zip code (20252). Since 1966 Smokey's been a regular balloon participant in Macy's Thanksgiving Day parade. In 1973 a float titled "How Green Was My Valley," featuring Smokey, won a blue ribbon in the Tournament of Roses Parade. And on his 40th birthday, in 1984, Smokey' s contribution to forest fire prevention was commemorated with a U.S. postage stamp designed by Rudolph Wendelin. Smokey's 50th anniversary in 1994 was celebrated all over the country with festivities, displays, and programs.

Smokey not only "advertises" the need for fire prevention but has also been connected with the advertising of firms and products such as Nabisco Shredded Wheat, Coca-Cola, Timberland Products Inc., Lever Brothers' "Aim Toothpaste," Winchell's Donut House, McCulloch chainsaws, Code One smoke alarms, the Johnson & Johnson Company, American Camper products, and a dozen or so others.

The Smokey story began in 1942 when shells from a Japanese submarine landed near a wooded area in Southern California. Although a fiery disaster was averted, Angeles National Forest officials realized they needed the public's help to safeguard the forest, as the war effort had thinned firefighters and equipment.

The Atlanta regional office of the United States Department of Agriculture (USDA) Forest Service got involved when they asked artist Harry Rossoll to devise a logo character. A stern-looking Ranger, a wooden creature called "fire devil," and a beaver (who would stamp out fire with his tail) were some of the nearly 100 ideas considered before a fuzzy bear with dungarees and a World War I campaign hat flowed from Rossoll's brush. At that point the U.S. Navy claimed Rossoll and he shipped out. Controversy surrounds whether Rossoll's bear concept ever reached the national office of the USDA Forest Service in Washington, D.C.

The newly-formed volunteer Wartime Advertising Council, when approached, designed a fire prevention ad campaign. In 1942 and 1943 the Council's first slogans appeared on posters and "car cards." The first forest animal poster, in 1944, featured Walt Disney's Bambi.

Shortly thereafter, it was (again) decided the campaign needed a forest animal symbol of its own. Artist Albert Staehle was commissioned to paint the first poster bear, shown pouring water on a campfire. Printed in 1944, the poster was distributed in 1945. The bear was named Smokey after "Smokey Joe" Martin, assistant fire chief of New York City's Fire Department from 1919 to 1930. Posters — as well as magazine, newspaper, and radio ads featuring Smokey Bear (clad in jeans, Forest Ranger's hat and badge, and carrying a shovel) — were heavily distributed nationwide. The late forest ranger/media team/script writer William "Bill" Bergoffen is credited as "the man who put the pants on Smokey Bear."

In 1950 a live bear cub with burned paws, found clinging to a tree following a forest fire near Capitan, New Mexico, was adopted by the USDA Forest Service. For the first six months or so he was called "Hot Foot Teddy" and then Smokey Bear. (Note: According to Rudy Wendelin, Smokey *the* Bear designation refers to the live Smokey Bear who lived at the National Zoo.) Smokey I lived at the National Zoo, Washington, D.C. until his death in 1976. The previous year he had been feted with a civil service retirement party, at the zoo, for 25 years of service. Smokey II, a black bear nicknamed "Little Smokey," resided at National Zoo until his death from liver cancer in 1990, aged 20. Smokey III died in 1992 and has not been replaced.

Smokey's activities have kept up with the times. In 1984 the U.S. Forest Service joined with the California Department of Forestry in a program called "Smokey and The Pros." Trading cards and posters featuring Smokey and baseball and football players got out Smokey's safety message. In the late 1980s a similar program, called "Smokey and the American Cowboy" was initiated, spotlighting top rodeo stars. And with the recent advent of "Mission HOME" (Harvesting Opportunity for Mother Earth), Smokey's educational efforts have expanded. He is now involved in space technology, nationally publicizing the down-to-earth benefits of space exploration, research, and development. Some of those benefits include the Forest Service's use of infrared and thermal scanners to fight wildfires, and weather forecasting and satellite-based remote sensing to help predict forest conditions and pinpoint locations for firefighters and slurry bombers.

Plush Smokey Bear: 1952 to 1999

Compiled by Fire Captain Richard C. Yokley, Bonita, California: Smokey Bear collector and researcher

The information contained in the following coverage of 15 different manufacturers from 1952 to 1999 is, to the best of my knowledge, accurate. It is based on visual inspection of collections, interviews, CFFP catalogs and annual reports, manufacturer records, and advertising data.

This list does not take into account the many prototypes made by various companies for licensing approval, and unlicensed or unauthorized bears. Dates of manufacture, style numbers, and original price of bears are unknown unless otherwise indicated. Dates shown are initial year of release. Prices noted are MSRP (manufacturer's suggested retail price) at the time of manufacture, during the time of sale. Price may be higher or lower depending on the retail outlet and its location. Secondary market values vary too greatly to be noted here.

Currently over 80 different plush bears have been identified, from Ideal's first issue in 1952 through Cooperstown Bears' 1999 Smokey.

1952-1953 Smokey Bear by Ideal, Bakelite vinyl resin head, hands, and feet. In 1952 Congress passed a bill allowing Ideal Toy Corporation exclusive right to make the first licensed Smokey Bear stuffed toy. *Photo courtesy of Fire Captain Richard C. Yokley.*

1953 Smokey Bear by Ideal, 26", Head mark: "© 1953, Smokey Says, Prevent Forest Fires, Ideal Toy Corp." *Photo courtesy of Kerra Davis.*

Ideal Toy Corporation, 1952-1971

General Characteristics: Ideal

Name: Smokey the Bear
Badge: Plastic, may be on right or left breast, says "Smokey Ranger, Prevent Forest Fires." In 1952, 1953, and 1954 may be in either metal or plastic.
Belt: Brown plastic, sewn to body at right and left hip.
Buckle: May be metal or plastic.(See badge.)
Eyes: Felt or plastic with moving pupils (googly), or amber plastic
Pants: Denim coloration may vary; most sitting bears have cuffed pants.
Feet: May be solid fur or fur toes and denim soles.
Paws: May be solid fur or two tone fur.
Talking: Pull string at right hip, in the back, or head; unknown manufacturer of mechanisms.
Manufacturer Tag: May be located on left or right thigh or left toe. 1952, 1953, and 1954 bears have tag on left hip at belt line. Tag says "Smokey," All other years are generic Ideal Toy Co. tags.

Ideal Smokeys with Numbers

The following bears were produced by the Ideal Toy Corporation of Hollis, New York.

1952. #7861 & 7862, issued at 14" & 22" standing, Bakelite vinyl resin head, hands and feet. Rest of body was brown rayon plush fur, with excelsior stuffing. Yellow felt hat with plastic band, removable denim twill pants, red or blue plastic shovel, plastic or metal buckle and badge, incised on back of head: "SMOKEY SAYS PREVENT FOREST FIRES, IDEAL TOY CORP." (No date.) Belt loops on 22" bear, half belt on 14" bear. Name on first box: "Ideal's Smokey "The Forest Fire Preventin' Bear."

In 1952 Smokey artist Rudolph Wendelin obtained fur from the Ideal Toy Corporation for the purpose of making a costume. Fur obtained was the fur being used in Ideal's Smokey the Bear doll issued in late 1952. This Smokey Bear costume was in Macy's Thanksgiving Day parade, and is now in Rudy Wendelin's private collection. (Mr. Wendelin was employed by the USDA Forest Service from 1937 to 1973. He has been involved with Smokey since 1946. In April, 1998, he was honored by the National Society Daughters of the American Revolution (NSDAR) with their highest award, the NSDAR Medal of Honor, for his "lasting contribution to our American heritage.")

1953. #7863 & #7864, 18" and 26" bear, same as 1952 bear described above except "1953" added to information incised on back of head. Wood handle on shovel; belt loops on 26" bear.

It is reported by various unconfirmed sources that a 26" Smokey Bear was given to President Dwight D. Eisenhower, who gave it to his grandson David. It was reported that the bear was given to the Smokey Bear Museum in Capitan, New Mexico. According to the museum director there is no record of any donation by David Eisenhower. The mu-

On right Smokey Bear by Ideal, head and body tag dated "© 1953." On left brown painted plastic Smokey Bear marked on the bottom "Art Line Inc, Chicago, IL, licensed." In the center 8-1/2" vinyl Smokey Bear by R. Dakin, 1967, #3535, Aim Toothpaste premium. *Courtesy of John & Shelley DeWitt, photo by Robert C. McDonald, Sr.*

seum obtained a 22" bear of this description for display in 1995, from a Florida donor. (Author's note: A 1953 photograph of President Eisenhower holding a large Ideal Smokey Bear, attributed to "Ideal publication courtesy of Mel Poretz," appears on page 117 of Judith Izen' s *Collector's Guide to Ideal Dolls*, published by Collector Books in 1994.)

1954. #7865, issued at 14", 17", and 18", all seated styles. Vinyl face, rust brown plush head and body. Two styles: (1) Bear with plastic buckle and badge has rust plush body, paws, and toes with denim soles. (2) Bear with metal buckle and badge has rust plush body, toes, and feet, beige paws. Belt may go around entire body, no belt loops. Original prices: 14" at $4.98, 17" Talking at $14.98, 18" at $6.98.

The 1954 17" bear is the first Talking Smokey. These were issued with a hand crank in Smokey's back, which activated a record in the bear's body playing several fire prevention messages. Various hat styles seen: a) Yellow plastic hat, band of rust colored ribbon with "Smokey" in white. b) Tan hat with red and white braid rope band, without name. c) Style #1 as indicated in the Knickerbocker section.

1955? 20", 22", and 25", seated bear, vinyl face, dark brown body and feet, beige paws, denim style pants. Style like 1954 issue.

1956. 14" and 18" seated bear, brown body and feet, beige toes, amber plastic eyes, badge on right breast, hat with painted on "Smokey" and band, plastic shovel.

1965. #7870-9, 26" seated bear, brown plush body, beige paws and soles of feet. Open mouth, red tongue, large black felt nose, felt eyes. Large brown felt hat with chin strap, denim cuffed pants, belt around body, belt loops, badge on left breast. Accessories: compass, whistle, and flashlight. Ideal 1965 catalog Sheet #8 called him "Large Cuddle Smokey." Weight 5 lbs.

1965. #7862-6, 14" sitting, dark brown body, toes, and feet. Beige muzzle and paws, dark brown felt nose and mouth, 9/16" amber eyes, badge on left breast, cuffed pants, manufacturer's tag on left leg at thigh. Bear came without hat or shovel. Ideal 1965 catalog Sheet #8 called him "Cuddle Smokey" and gave his weight as *12 lbs.* (probably a misprint.)

1965. #7866-7, 19" sitting, same as above bear except 5/8" amber eyes, issued with shovel and thick plastic hat with chin strap. Badge on left breast. Ideal 1965 catalog Sheet #8 called him "Cuddle Smokey" also and gave his weight as 2 lbs..

1967. #7875-8, 13" bear stands, brown plush body and toes, beige paws, denim soles, manufacturer's tag on left toe. Badge on left breast. 3/4" plastic amber eyes, hat with stick-on label name, black felt nose, red felt tongue.

1967. #7863-4, 12" same as above. Also issued in 14" and 16" sizes (unknown style numbers), 16" issue priced at $3.98, "for ages 2 through 7." The 14" also comes in a Talking version with pull string at left shoulder.

1969. #7891-5, Talker, 16" seated bear, brown body, toes and feet, beige paws, badge on left breast, manufacturer's tag on lower left leg, hat with stick-on label name "Talking" with pull string at right hip.

There are two versions of the Ideal talking mechanisms. It is unknown when the change took place.

Version One messages:

1. "Hi, I'm Smokey The Bear.
2. See my ranger badge
3. Help Prevent Forest Fires
4. (Bird whistle) There's a whippoorwill
5. Don't play with matches
6. I love all boys and girls
7. I'm a cuddly bear
8. The animals are my friends.
9. (Bird whistle) There's a robin.
10. C'mon, give me a bear hug.
11. I'm the fire fightin' bear
12. I live in the friendly forest."

Version Two messages:

1. "Hi, I'm Smokey The Bear
2. Help prevent forest fires.
3. I live in the friendly forest.
4. See my ranger badge.
5. (Bird whistle) There's a whippoorwill.
6. Don't play with matches.
7. I like all boys and girls.
8. I'm a cuddly bear.
9. Forest animals are my friends.
10. (Noise) That's a rabbit.
11. Come on, give me a bear hug
12. I'm the fire fighting bear."

The pull strings are located at the right hip, or in the back, or the back of the head.

It was thought that the post code may help date the bears as the zone 2 digit codes were used from 1945 to 1963 when the 5 digit Zip Code began. However, Ideal's manufacturer tags utilize the zone code throughout their manufacturing period or used tags with no address at all. Knickerbocker bears all use the zip code.

Belt buckles on all Smokey bears are standard size, 7/8" x 2-1/2", gray color plastic, unless otherwise indicated.

Height measurements on Ideal and Knickerbocker bears may vary an inch or even more as stuffing shifts and settles with age and/or if bear was vigorously played with.

Ideal Smokeys of Unknown Date

Date Unknown. 13" seated, brown plush body, head and toes, beige paws, denim soles, two styles of vinyl muzzle; open and closed mouth, 3/8" amber eyes, badge on left breast.

Date Unknown. 13" seated, cinnamon brown plush body, head, toes and feet, beige paws, blue cotton (not denim) pants and soles. Open vinyl muzzle with mouth in a "kiss" look rather than full open (as above bears). Longer torso and shorter legs than above bears, to achieve the same height. Amber eyes with beige or white felt behind, smaller black nose than above style with visible nostrils.

Date Unknown. 14" same as above except 1/2" amber eyes and "MFG22" tag on right leg at thigh.

Date Unknown. 14" seated, brown body, toes and feet, beige muzzle and paws, badge on right breast, dark brown felt nose and mouth, black felt eyes, cuffed pants, manufacturer tag on left leg at thigh.

Date Unknown. 15" seated, brown body, toes and feet, beige muzzle and paws, badge on left breast, black felt nose, red felt tongue, 5/8" amber plastic eyes, non-cuffed pants, manufacturer tag on left thigh.

Date Unknown. 18", seated bear, light brown body, toes and feet, beige muzzle and paws, black felt eyes, brown felt nose, red felt tongue, badge on right breast, manufacturer tag on left thigh.

Date Unknown. 19" seated bear, light brown body, feet and toes, beige muzzle and paws, plastic googly eyes, brown felt nose and mouth, badge on right breast, cuffed pants, manufacturer tag on right thigh.

Date Unknown. 19" seated bear, light brown body, feet and toes, beige muzzle and paws, 1/2" amber eyes, brown felt nose and mouth, cuffed pants, badge on right breast, manufacturer tag on right thigh.

Date Unknown. 19", sitting, same as above except manufacturer's tag on left thigh.

Closeup of vinyl mask face (with open mouth), 1954 Smokey Bear by Ideal. *Author's collection.*

Two vinyl mask face Ideal Smokey Bears of 1954 with rust plush fur. Smokey on left has plush soles and metal belt buckle and badge. Smokey on right has denim soles with plastic belt buckle and badge. Original prices for 1954 Ideal Smokey were 14": $.4.98; 18": $6.98; and 17" Talking at $14.98. *Photo courtesy of Fire Captain Richard C. Yokley.*

18" Ideal Smokey Bear of 1954, missing tag, belt, badge, hat, and shovel. $35-$100. *Author's collection.*

Ideal Smokey Bear with one hooded eye and felt eyelashes, circa 1950s. *Photo courtesy of Kerra Davis.*

Seated Ideal Smokey, circa 1956 with "Ideal's Wonderful Toy" tag. Standing Ideal Smokey Bear, circa 1950s, plastic hooded inset eyes with black felt eyelashes, tag: "Smokey, Official licensee authorized by the U.S. Department of Agriculture, Prevent Forest Fires, Made by Ideal." (Standing bear is not included in the Plush Smokeys List.) *Courtesy of John & Shelley DeWitt, Photo by Robert C. MacDonald, Sr.*

1965 Ideal 26" "Large Cuddle Smokey" #7870-9. Accessories are whistle around neck, compass and flashlight hooked to belt, hat and badge. Pants are cuffed. Photo from Ideal Toy Corporation 1965 sales sheet. *Courtesy of Fire Captain Richard Yokley.*

1965 Ideal 19" "Cuddle Smokey" with shovel, hat, and badge. Photo from Ideal Toy Corporation 1965 sales sheet. *Courtesy of Fire Captain Richard Yokley.*

1965 Ideal 14" "Cuddle Smokey," came only with badge and belt. Badge reads: "Smokey / Ranger / Prevent / Forest Fires." "Smokey" on belt is in large print. Photo from Ideal Toy Corporation 1965 sales sheet. *Courtesy of Fire Captain Richard Yokley.*

Two sizes of 1967 Ideal Smokeys, tag on right toe. *Courtesy of Fire Captain Richard C. Yokley.*

13" standing Ideal Smokey, 1967, plastic badge and belt buckle, tag on right toe: "It's a Wonderful Toy, Made in USA, IDEAL, Ideal Toy Corp., Hollis 23, NY." Tag reverse: "Surface washable, All new material, Do not submerge." (Generic Ideal tag rather than Smokey tag.) Hat and shovel are not original. *Author's collection.*

Knickerbocker Toy Company, 1971-1977

Knickerbocker Toy Company of Middlesex, New Jersey manufactured their Smokey bears in Japan, Haiti, and Taiwan from 1971 to 1977. The place of manufacture can be determined by the color of the tag: blue for Japan, green for Haiti, and brown for Taiwan.

Hats. There are at least two hat styles, both of yellow plastic: (1) Heavy plastic, 1 millimeter thick, brown hat band painted on at 1/2" wide, outlining "Smokey" name. (2) Thin plastic, 1/50" thick with no hat band. Name is applied via yellow sticker that is 13/16" x 2-1/2", with name in various shades of brown. It is unknown which style of hat goes on which bear (Ideal or Knickerbocker) unless an "in box" or photo can identify. Hats were held in place with thin white plastic cord that went under the chin.

Badges. The metal shield style badge measuring 1-3/4" across the top and 2-1/8" top to bottom that says "Junior Forest Ranger," with a likeness of Smokey (in the center of the badge) looking to his right or straight ahead, and the words "Prevent Forest Fires" along the bottom of the badge are NOT the original badges that came with the bears. This style badge came in the Junior Forest Ranger kit and could only be obtained by a written request to Smokey Headquarters, Washington, D.C.

General Characteristics: Knickerbocker

Name: Smokey Bear
Badge: Plastic, located on right or left breast, says "Smokey Ranger" with a likeness of Smokey looking to his left
Belt: Brown plastic, sewn to body at hips
Buckle: Gray plastic, 7/8" x 2-1/2"
Eyes: Amber plastic, or felt, or black plastic with felt

Closeup of Berryman style face, Smokey Bear, 1972 by Knickerbocker. In the 1940s Cliff Berryman was an artist with the Wartime Forest Fire Prevention campaign.

Manufacturer Tag: On left or right hip, many say "Smokey Bear." Tag colors are blue for Japan, green for Haiti, and brown for Taiwan.

Pants: Denim, coloration varies, none are cuffed.

Face: Two styles, Berryman and Standard

Talker: Pull string at various locations, 12 phrases, unknown manufacturer of mechanisms.

Knickerbocker Smokeys with "Berryman" Style Faces

A U.S. Forest Service memo dated August 9, 1944, regarding "artwork" for the Wartime Forest Fire Prevention campaign specified that one of the requirements on the subject "characterization of the bear" was that a Cliff Berryman-style face was NOT to be used. We do, however, see it in the early Knickerbocker bears listed below.

1972. #9821, 6" standing all fabric bear with box

1972. #1502, Talker, 14" stands, dark brown body, paws, and toes, denim soles, badge on right breast, hat with stick-on label with name in red or light brown, black button eyes with felt, talks with pull string at right hip.

Date and Number Unknown. 24" sitting, dark brown fur body, paws, and toes, denim soles, beige muzzle, black button eyes, badge on left breast, large belt buckle at 1-5/8" x 4".

Date and Number Unknown. 30" standing bear, large badge at 2-1/4" x 2-1/4", all other information same as the 24" bear above.

Date and Number Unknown. 14" sitting bear, dark brown body, paws, and toes, beige face, denim soles, denim pants not cuffed, black plastic button eyes with brown and white felt surrounding the eye, black felt nose, light brown felt mouth, red felt tongue, badge on right breast, manufacturer's tag on left hip.

Date and Number Unknown. 11" sitting bear, dark brown body, paws, and toes, beige face, denim soles, denim pants not cuffed, black plastic button eyes with brown and white felt surrounding the eyes, black felt nose, light brown felt mouth, red felt tongue, badge on right breast, manufacturer's tag on left leg near belt.

Date and Number Unknown. 11" sitting, same as 11" bear above except badge on left breast and manufacturer's tag on right hip.

Date and Number Unknown. Talker, 11" sitting, dark brown body, paws, and toes, beige face, denim soles, denim pants not cuffed, black plastic button eyes with brown and white felt surrounding eyes, black felt nose, light brown felt mouth, red felt tongue, badge may be on right or left breast, manufacturer's tag on left leg near belt, pull string through belt at right hip.

The talking Knickerbocker bears were issued with 12 phrases. Knickerbocker Talking Smokey messages (1971-1977):

1. Hi, there. I'm Smokey Bear.
2. I'm a soft cuddly bear.
3. I love all girls and boys.
4. Forest animals are my friends.
5. See my ranger badge and hat.
6. Show me to your friends.
7. Help prevent forest fires.
8. Don't play with matches.
9. Camping is great fun.
10. How about a bear hug?
11. How old are you?
12. Let's enjoy the outdoors.

Seated Knickerbocker Smokey Bear with Berryman face, circa 1971, badge on left side. *Photo courtesy of Fire Captain Richard C. Yokley.*

Standing Knickerbocker pull string Talker Smokey Bear with Berryman face, circa 1972, badge on right side. *Photo courtesy of Kerra Davis.*

From 1972 all cloth 6" Smokey Bear with a Berryman face. His waist tag reads: "The Official SMOKEY BEAR, Licensed U.S. Forest Service." Tag reverse: "KTC, Knickerbocker, © Knickerbocker Toy Co Inc., Middlesex, NJ, USA, Made in Taiwan."

14" standing Berryman-faced Knickerbocker Talker Smokey Bear. Pull string comes through ring in belt. Badge with Smokey face on right chest. *Author's collection.*

Knickerbocker Smokeys with the Standard Face Style

The following listed bears are all of the "Standard Face" style, as the Knickerbocker Company changed face styles to the version made popular with the Ideal Toy Company. It is unknown just exactly when this took place.

Date Unknown. #1400, 14" sitting, rust plush body, paws, and toes, denim soles, beige muzzle, black felt nose, red felt tongue, amber plastic eyes, badge on right breast, manufacturer's tag on left hip, hat with sticker label.

Date Unknown. #1402, 14" standing bear, brown body, paws, and toes, denim feet, beige muzzle, amber eyes, black felt nose, red felt tongue, badge on left breast, manufacturer's tag on right hip, hat with sticker name.

Date Unknown. #1500, Talker, 10" sitting, light brown body, paws, and toes, denim soles, amber plastic eyes, beige muzzle, black felt nose, red felt tongue, badge on left breast, hat with sticker name, pull string at left waist or hip.

Date Unknown. Cal-T-5 - Talker, 14" standing, brown body and toes, beige muzzle and paws, denim soles, amber plastic eyes, black felt nose, red felt tongue, badge on left breast, pull string at right waist, tag in back seam at waist, half belt, plastic buckle Tag says: "The Official// SMOKEY BEAR// Help Prevent Forest Fires//Cal-T-5// All New Cotton and Foam" Tag reverse: "KTC// Knickerbocker/ / ©Knickerbocker Toy Company, Inc// Middlesex, N.J. 08846, U.S.A.//Surface Washable//Sewn in Haiti." (This listing added by the author.)

Date and Number Unknown. Talker, 16" standing, dark brown body and toes, beige muzzle and paws, black felt nose, red felt tongue, amber plastic eyes, denim soles, badge on left breast, pull string through belt on left side.

Date and Number Unknown. Talker, 16" standing, dark brown body and toes, beige muzzle and paws, denim soles, plastic eyes with "see-through" Iris, stitched mouth, no tongue, badge on right breast, pull string at right or left hip.

Date and Number Unknown. Talker, 16" sitting bear, dark brown body, toes, and paws, beige muzzle, amber plastic eyes, denim soles, black felt nose, red felt tongue, badge on left breast, manufacturer's tag in bears back at waist, pull string on left side through belt.

Date and Number Unknown. 14" standing bear, dark brown body and toes, beige muzzle and paws, denim soles, black felt nose, red felt tongue, 5/8" plastic eyes with "see through" Iris, badge on left breast, brown manufacturer' s tag on right hip says "Official Smokey Bear"

Date and Number Unknown. 15" (or 16") sitting bear, brown body and toes, beige muzzle and paws, denim soles, black felt nose, red felt tongue, 5/8" plastic eyes with black Iris, badge (?), blue manufacturer's tag on right hip.

Date and Number Unknown. 16" sitting bear, rust brown body and toes, beige muzzle and paws, denim soles, black felt nose, red felt tongue, 11/16" plastic eyes with "see through" Iris, badge on right breast, brown manufacturer' s tag on left hip says "Official Smokey Bear"

Date and Number Unknown. 24" standing bear, dark brown body and toes, beige muzzle and paws, denim soles, black felt nose, red felt tongue, 7/8" amber plastic eyes, badge on left breast, manufacturer's tag unknown.

Date and Number Unknown. 24" standing bear, dark brown plush body and feet, beige muzzle and paws, denim soles, amber plastic eyes, black felt nose, red felt tongue, hat size larger than standard (unknown size), name applied via sticker, badge on left breast, location of manufacturer's tag unknown.

Date and Number Unknown. 32" standing bear, dark brown plush body and feet, denim soles, beige muzzle and paws, 5/16" amber eyes, red felt tongue, black felt nose, large yellow hat with sticker name, large badge on left breast 2-1/4" x 2-1/8", large buckle 1-5/8" x 4-3/8"

Date and Number Unknown. 36" standing bear, dark brown plush body and feet, beige muzzle and paws, denim soles, amber eyes, red felt tongue, black felt nose, large yellow hat, sticker name, large badge on left breast: 2-1/4" x 2-1/4", large buckle: 1-5/8" x 4"

14" well loved Knickerbocker pull string Talker Smokey Bear with standard face. Badge on left chest, pull string comes from right waist. Back seam tag: "The Official SMOKEY BEAR, Help Prevent Forest Fires, Cal-T-5, All New Cotton and Foam." Tag reverse: "KTC, Knickerbocker, © Knickerbocker Toy Company, Inc., Middlesex, NJ 08846, USA, Surface washable, Sewn in Haiti." The tag number on this Smokey is a newly discovered one. *Courtesy of Linda Hildebrant.*

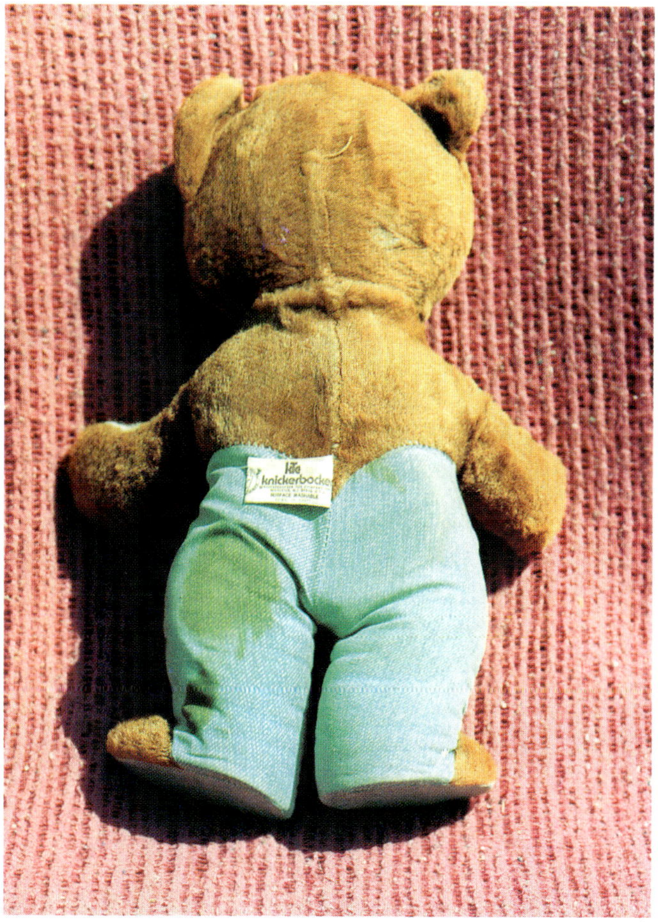

Back view of 14" plush Knickerbocker Talker Smokey, showing his tag and beltless back. His hat is missing. *Courtesy of Linda Hildebrant.*

Unknown Manufacturer

Date Unknown. 8-1/2" sitting bear, cinnamon or light brown plush body and tops of feet, denim foot soles, sewn on denim style pants, no belt loops, red felt nose, 3/8" amber plastic eyes, mouth type unknown, no badge, red plastic belt 5/16" wide goes around body and says "LITTLE SMOKEY" in white letters on belt front, tag information unknown.

8-1/2" Little Smokey by unknown manufacturer, with red belt and denim soles. *Courtesy of Fire Captain Richard C. Yokley.*

R. Dakin Company, 1971-1985

The R. Dakin Company of San Francisco produced plush Smokeys (with no badges) made in Korea and standing vinyl Smokey figures made in Hong Kong. Most of the vinyl bears predated Dakin's plush Smokeys.

General Characteristics: R. Dakin

Hats for the 1977, and 1980 through 1985 Dakin Smokey plush bears are held in place with 1/8" brown plastic band or brown cord that goes under the chin.

R. Dakin Smokey bears made from 1980 to 1985 had these common characteristics: Tan plastic hat with stick-on name label with name in various shades of brown. Buckles were standard size in 1980; in other years they were 1/2" x 1-1/4". Belt was black leatherette, sewn in the back. They were made in Korea.

R. Dakin's Plush Smokeys

1977. T Shirt Smokey, #31-2621 (same style number for all colors) - Green shirt says "Think". This message was also seen on a blue shirt. Yellow shirt says "I think I love you Smokey Bear." White shirt has red printing with a red heart, says "I (heart) Smokey." Shirts were sewn to the body and are not removable. Bears are 14" standing, with dark fur body, paws, and feet, beige muzzle, no badge, hat tan plastic with yellow stick-on name "Smokey," belt tan fabric sewn permanently or with Velcro® closure, made in Korea, issue price $14.98.

1980. #31-1284, 14" standing bear, dark brown fur body and feet, red tag back of left foot, issue price $11.00.

1983. #28-0015, 10" standing bear, dark brown fur body and feet, red tag back of left foot, issue price $9.00.

1983. Number unknown, 12" standing bear, dark brown fur body and feet, 1983 value $13.95, used in a promotion for Code One smoke detectors made by Jameson Home Products

1985. #31-1196, 12" sitting bear, cinnamon fur body, tan feet, blue tag on left buttocks, issue price $14.00.

1985. #31-1196, 13" sitting bear, cinnamon fur body and feet, blue tag on left buttocks, issue price $10.98.

R. Dakin Vinyl Smokeys, 1967-1985

In addition to making plush Smokeys, R. Dakin from 1967 to 1985 produced a series of standing vinyl Smokeys which were made in Hong Kong. Although they are not plush, they are included in this section for your information:

1967. #3535, 8-1/2" all vinyl body and hat, brown body, yellow hat is glued on, removable denim pants, brass buckle, separate shovel says "Prevent Forest Fires" on the blade. Two versions were made: (1) poseable head, arms, and legs. (2) poseable head and arms only. These were offered through Lever Brothers Aim Toothpaste coupons, and in 1985 in a Johnson & Johnson promotion. The style was also used on banks, desk sets, and other items.

1973. #5035, 4-1/2" hard plastic body, hands molded to side, no shovel, non-poseable. It came in Tonka set of three U.S.F.S. (green) fire vehicles with ranger and animals. Set was titled "Smokey Bear & His Forest Friends."

1974. Number Unknown, 5-1/4" all vinyl Squeaker Toy.

1976. #13-3589, 6-3/4" hard vinyl, R. Dakin TV, poseable head, arms, and waist, name "Smokey the Bear"

14" standing T-Shirt plush Smokey Bears by R. Dakin, 1977. Shirts are part of their bodies. Another T-Shirt Smokey was made in a white shirt, saying "I (red heart) Smokey." *Photo courtesy of Fire Captain Richard C. Yokley.*

14" standing plush Smokey Bear, by R. Dakin 1980. Attached to his hand is a 1984 First Day Issue of the 20 cent Smokey Bear stamp. Manufacturer tag on rear foot says "Product of Korea." Paper tag gives style #31-1284, date 1980, and suggests "Join Smokey Bear Junior Ranger Club….." Condition Mint with tag. Value: $50-$60. *Courtesy of Bonnie and Larry Vaughan.*

Plush Smokey Bears by R. Dakin, 1980-1985. The bears on left and right almost have Berryman faces. Note that their feet are different from each other. *Photo courtesy of Fire Captain Richard C. Yokley.*

8-1/2" molded brown vinyl Smokey wearing removable dark blue denim jeans with cuffs. Soft plastic head, arms and head move, legs have joint mark but are not movable. Metal "Smokey" belt buckle; plastic shovel says "Prevent Forest Fires." Notice short shovel handle with shovel pointing down. Pants tag: "Smokey Bear, R. Dakin & Co, San Francisco, Prod. of Hong Kong." Paper tag: "Official Licensee, Cooperative Forest Fire Prevention Program, Authorized by U.S.C. 711." Tag reverse: "R. Dakin & Co, San Francisco, No. 2275, Smokey Bear, Prod. of Hong Kong." Foot mark: "© R. Dakin & Co, Authorized user, San Francisco, Product of Hong Kong." Circa 1967-1985. The number 2275 and short handled down pointing shovel are different from others seen. *Courtesy of Nancy Vanselow.*

Back view of 8-1/2" vinyl R. Dakin Smokey showing tags, back belt, and pants closure. *Courtesy of Nancy Vanselow.*

8-1/2" molded brown vinyl Smokey dressed in twill jeans with cuffs, holds long handled shovel with shovel pointing up. Yellow plastic hat. Tag reads "R. Dakin & Co, #3535, product of Hong Kong." Purchased with coupons from Lever Brothers Aim Toothpaste. Circa 1967. *Courtesy of Oneida Callaway, photo by Mary Ann Callaway Dennis.*

Fun Farm, 1978

Fun Farm of San Francisco, in 1978, made a plush Smokey which was produced in Korea.

1978. 11" standing bear, dark brown body, paws, and feet, beige muzzle, 5/8" amber eyes with white felt behind the eyes, black open mouth, black plastic nose with nostrils, light brown leatherette belt, yellow paper buckle same as for hat label, tan hat with stick-on label name, no badge, pants of blue fabric sewn to body. Two manufacturer's tags: (1) in back at belt line, (2) inside left foot seam. Issue price $7.99.

11" standing plush Smokey Bear by Fun Farm, 1978. Issue price was $7.99. *Photo courtesy of Fire Captain Richard C. Yokley.*

ITI Hawaii, 1979

Although the company name is ITI Hawaii, it is actually located in Korea and the bears were manufactured in Korea.

1979. Clip-On, 1-1/2", 3", and 4" standing bear, pinch at shoulders for clipping to objects such as car mirror; yellow plastic hat, denim pants, dark brown fur body and feet, beige muzzle, brown leatherette hat band with "Smokey" in white, brown leatherette belt with yellow leatherette buckle with "Smokey" in dark brown, poseable head. Some of the 3" and 4" bears have a loop in the right paw to hold a shovel similar to Dakin's 1972 plastic shovel, but this shovel is smaller. Issue price for 3" and 4" was $3.98.

Three Bears Inc., 1985-1989

Three Bears Inc. of Sedona, Arizona and Newport, Rhode Island produced Smokeys made in Korea from 1985 to 1989.

General Characteristics: Three Bears Inc.

Name: Smokey
Hat: Floppy and stiff brim
Belt: Tan fabric, sewn all around body
Buckle: Yellow fabric sewn to belt
Tail: These are the only Smokeys with a tail, pants slit in back to reveal tail
Pants: Removable on 15" and 30", all denim and cuffed
Paws: 15" and 30" beige, 6" and 12" solid brown
Feet: 6", 15" and 30" beige; 12" solid brown
Manufacturer's Tag: 6", 12", and 15" on left hip, 30" on left leg near foot. Tags for all sizes except the 12" bear read: "Newport, RI". Tag for 12" bear with floppy hat says: "Sedona, AZ."

Three Bears Smokeys

1985. #SB-06-1, 6" bear, sitting, Christmas ornament, issue price $5.00

1985. SB 15 1, 15" bear, sitting, issue price $28.00

1985. SB-30-1, 30" bear, sitting, issue price $99.00

1989/1990. SB-12-1, 12" or 12-1/2" bear sitting, initial offering through Johnson & Johnson Co. coupon program. Slight variations to later general release of the 12" bear may be due to the manufacturing process, and not necessarily due to style changes.

Advertising sheet for Three Bears Inc. © 1987. The 30" size bear is #SB-30-1, 15" size is #SB-15-1, and 6" size is #SB-06-1. The jeans of the two larger sizes are removable. The smaller one was intended as a Christmas ornament. None of the bears came boxed. *Courtesy of Fire Captain Richard Yokley.*

12" sitting brown plush Smokey with beige snout and paw pads. Jeans are part of body; cuffed jeans have back pocket, tail protrudes through jeans. Brown flannel sewn-on belt with gold fabric "buckle" embroidered SMOKEY. Soft velour hat with "Smokey" on front. Plastic eyes, dark brown velour nose. Tag at belt back: "© Three Bears, Inc., Sedona, AZ 86336, Made in Korea." Folded paper tag attached to left ear: Front (Smokey head) "A portion of this sale given to the US Forest Service for Fire prevention, Smokey" Inside left: "Free Smokey Bear Junior Forest ranger Kit, Write: Smokey Bear, Washington, DC, 20252." Inside right: (seal with Smokey head) "Official Licensee Cooperative Forest Fire Prevention Program. Remember, Only YOU Can Prevent Forest Fires!, Smokey (paw print). Back: "Three Bears (bear) Inc, Sedona, AZ 86336, (bar code), Style #SB-1-2-1, Care Surface washable, © 1985, Made in Korea." This bear was obtained by sending in Band-Aid sales slips in the Johnson & Johnson promotion of 1990. The style number and date are new discoveries. *Courtesy of Shirley Taylor.*

Plush Smokey Bears made by Three Bears, Inc. during 1985 to 1989. The "Little Smokey" perching on the big bear's hat is 6" seated. His body and head are round and firm. In 1985, year of issue, price was $5.00. *Photo courtesy of Fire Captain Richard C. Yokley.*

1994 advertising piece for J.J. Wind Inc.'s 23" 50th Anniversary Smokey wearing cuffed jeans, belt, hat, and holding shovel. Note he has no badge.

J.J. Wind, 1994-1998

J.J. Wind of North Bergen, New Jersey, produced their Smokey bears in Indonesia. All hangtags are dated 1994 regardless of year of release.

1994. #SM1009CC, 23" standing bear in "Special Limited Edition" box with 50th anniversary sticker on box. Dark brown body and feet, beige muzzle, pink open mouth, plastic nose, removable denim pants have snap and zipper front, metal buckle on brown leather belt with Velcro® closure, hat light brown felt with silk screen name in dark brown, leather hat band; no badge, hangtag in left ear says "50th Anniversary 1994" (in 1994 only). Manufacturer's tag inside left foot. Large painted wood shovel. Issue price in box $45.95, without box $39.95.

1995. Same bear as above except no 50th anniversary emblems and some of the shovels may be unpainted.

1998. #SM00003CC, 12" and 16" standing, identical to the 23" except smaller size, unpainted shovels

1998. #SM00020FP, 6" finger puppet, same description as above except no shovel, pants not cuffed or removable

23" "Special Limited Edition Smokey Bear" by J.J. Wind, 1994, in 50th Anniversary box. Brown plush Smokey holds wooden shovel. Tag: "Remember 50, Smokey has for 50 years." *Courtesy of Nancy Vanselow.*

Back view of Smokey's 50th Anniversary box lists Smokey's Rules. The first letters of each line spell his name vertically. *Courtesy of Nancy Vanselow.*

Raikes Bears, 1994 (50th Anniversary)

The bears of Robert Raikes of Catalina, Arizona are highly collectible and notable for their carved wooden faces and superior quality. The following bear is not approved nor licensed by the U.S.F.S. for production. Although not licensed, the bear is noted here as the U.S.F.S. took seven bears for their own use.

1994. 42" sitting bear with wooden face, paws and feet, dark brown fur body, straw hat, leather belt with metal "Smokey" buckle, denim pants, no badge. Limited edition of 15 for 50th anniversary was not for sale. Distribution was as follows: 7 to U.S.F.S. for distribution (which included 1 to California Mobile Smokey Bear Museum and 1 to Smokey Bear Historical State Park, Capitan, New Mexico, other 5 unknown destinations); 1 auctioned in Japan for $8,500; 4 raffled: 1 each in Toledo, Ohio, Boxborough, Massachusetts, San Diego, California, and Raikes Collectors Club; 1 (Raikes Smokey #4) on display at Teddy Bear Museum in Naples, Florida; 1 on display at Raikes Collectors Club in Mt. Shasta, California, and 1 in Robert Raikes personal collection.

Raikes Originals, 1996

1996. Hot Foot Teddy - 16" sitting bear cub with wood face, paws and feet, variegated light and dark brown fur, bandaged left paw with left arm in sling, bandaged left foot. No hat, pants, badge or belt buckle. Made in China. Wood hangtag attached to right foot reads: "Robert Raikes Hot Foot Teddy." All bears are signed and numbered, edition limited to 500 bears, issue price $125.00. Bear not licensed by U.S.F.S. as a Smokey bear item. Approved by the Hot Foot Teddy Collectors Association for use of the name. A portion of the sale of each bear is returned to the Association by Mr. Raikes.

Colos International IBTT/ In Toy F.E. LTD/Bon Ton Toys, Inc., 1992-1996

The company is located in Dayton, New Jersey and Hong Kong and the bears are manufactured in China.

General Characteristics

Name: Smokey Bear
Badge: None
Belt: Brown leatherette
Buckle: Dark brown felt with "Smokey" in yellow
Hat: Felt, light brown, silk screen name and felt band dark brown,
Body: Dark brown body and feet, light brown plush soles, beige muzzle
Mouth: Closed
Nose: Plastic
Eyes: Almond shape, brown plastic around eyes
Shovel: with all bears except 8" bear
Manufacturer's Tag: Bon Ton Toys located inside left leg under cuffed denims, 8" bear outside of pants
Hangtag: "In Toys F.E. Ltd," on left paw, 50th Anniversary tag in 1994 only

Height of the following bears includes the hat. Measurements are the official sizes from the "Colos International Bon Ton Toy Co."

1994 Limited Edition of 15 made by Robert Raikes for Smokey's 50th anniversary was not for sale. Seven went to the USDA Forest Service, several went to museums, others to be auctioned (raffled). The 42" sitting bear has wooden face, paws and feet, dark brown fur body, straw hat, leather belt with brass "Smokey" buckle, denim pants, no badge. The Teddy Bear Museum is proud to own #4 with its certificate. *Courtesy of George B. Black, Jr., Teddy Bear Museum of Naples, Florida.*

Plush Smokey Bears from Bon Ton Toys Inc, 1994. *Photo courtesy of Fire Captain Richard C. Yokley.*

1992. 8" standing "Cuddle and Color" bear printed on fabric, for ages 3 and up, 6 color pens included in package, color, wash, and color again Came in clear see-through package.

1994. #SB-8, 8" standing bear, no shovel, issue price $9.00

1994. #SB-125, 12-1/2" standing bear, issue price $20.00

1994. #SB-125, 12-1/2" standing bear in 50th Anniversary box, only 4800 "in box", distributed mainly on the East Coast, issue price $12.97

1994. #SB-135, Talker, 13-1/2" standing bear, says 4 phrases: (1) Only you can prevent forest fires., (2) Be careful with matches and campfires. (3) Respect the forest, protect our trees. (4) My friends depend on me.), electronically produced by battery, exclusively sold through J.C. Penney catalogs, issue price $19.98

1994. #SB-155, 15-1/2" standing bear, issue price $30.00

1995. Talker, bear available from Sears and J.C. Penney

1996. Talker, bear available by general issue; issue prices: Sears & J.C. Penney $19.98, others $39.95

In July 1997 at the 23rd annual Coca-Cola® Convention held in Colorado Springs, Colorado, the 1994 issue of the Bon Ton bears was utilized as part of their promotional giveaways. Using 1960s vintage advertising, the 12-1/2" bear and 15" bear were packaged in a box utilizing 1960s artwork featuring Smokey with the two cubs carrying a basket of food and Coke. The boxes and bears are individually numbered with bears having numbered Coke hangtags and Bon Ton 50th anniversary and manufacturer's tags. The 12-1/2" bear was issued at 400 units; the 15" bear was issued at 2,000 units. Only 60 of the 8" bears were made to be used as centerpieces. With their 50th anniversary (1994) tags still attached, they were put into small pails with flowers. Since the small bear did not have a shovel, a branding iron, whose end was shaped like a Coke bottle, was made to put in his paw. Also issued for the convention were Smokey/Coke items such as 2,000 serving trays, 2050 decks of playing cards, and 972 T-shirts. All of these items used the same artwork of Harry Rossoll, who created "Smokey Bear's Story of the Forest."

Bon Ton Toys, Inc., 1996

This Smokey was only sold boxed with the book "A Story of Smokey Bear" issue priced at $15.99. He has no badge, shovel or hangtag.

1996. #SB-9, 9" standing bear, cinnamon brown fur body, beige muzzle and soles of feet, open pink mouth, felt nose, brown leatherette around plastic eyes. Pants are denim, sewn to body, with single stitch side seams. Belt is brown leatherette with felt "Smokey" buckle in yellow. Hat is tan with brown felt hat band, "Smokey" in light brown. Manufacturer's tag is inside left leg; made in China.

Above: Advertising sheet for Colos International Co. Inc.'s Smokey SB-125 (on left) and SB-155 (on right). Note felt footpads and small spades on shovels. *Courtesy of Fire Captain Richard Yokley.*

Left: A plush Talking Smokey Bear by Colos International/Bon Ton, initially released in 1994. Squeeze his paw and he reminds you, "Remember only you can prevent forest fires!" He has three other (a total of 4) fire prevention messages. Issue price: $19.98. The 1996 catalog price was $39.95 *Photo courtesy of Michael Kruckenberg.*

Kids Preferred Inc., 1997-1998

Kids Preferred Inc. is the new name for "Colos International." Bon Ton Toy Company name changed due to similar name usage in Holland by their sister company. The firm is located in Dayton, New Jersey and manufactures its bears in China. This 8" bear at first glance resembles Bon Ton' s 1994 small 8" bear. The differences are as follows:

1997. Style Number Unknown, 8" standing bear, dark fur body, black felt nose, dark brown felt soles, no stitching on paws of feet, almond shaped eyes with black plastic around them, pants have single stitching on outside seam, the belt buckle is larger than the Bon Ton bears and the name is in smaller print. Manufacturer's tag on left leg reads: "Kids Preferred Inc." and hangtag says "For Ages 3 and Up."

On the following Kids Preferred Smokeys, all hangtags use the old "In Toys F.E. Ltd" logo and are dated 1994 regardless of date of issue. The sewn-in manufacturer's tags are actual year dated with the new company name "Kids Preferred".

1997. 6-1/2" sitting bean bag bear, brown velour body and feet, soles of feet (almost) olive drab color in velour, beige muzzle with sewn on black nose and mouth, denim style cuffed pants, leatherette belt with brown felt buckle with "Smokey" in yellow, attached tan hat with felt hat band and "Smokey" in brown on hat. Manufacturer' s tag on left leg on outside seam dated 1997, hangtags on left arm.

1997. 5-1/4" standing, same style as beanbag bear. Has metal chain-link chain attached at neck with a key chain holder at the end. Manufacturer's tag at rear of bear dated 1997

1998. 6-1/2" sitting bean bag bear identical to the 1997 issue with the following exceptions: (1) Christmas issue with "Christmas 1998" hangtag, (2) Red ribbon sewn to left leg with "Christmas 1998" in black on ribbon. Manufacturer's tag sewn to bear's bottom is dated "1998." Released in limited edition of 6,000.

1998. 6-1/2" sitting bean bag bear, identical to 1997 issue with the exception that a gray plastic shovel, approximately 3" long, is included with bear. Manufacturer' s tag sewn to left leg, dated "1998." Edition limited to 200 units.

Northern Gifts Inc., 1998

Northern Gifts Inc. of Blaine, Washington offered four small Smokey Bears made in Indonesia.

1998. #06100 9" bear, sitting, issue price $8.00 each
1998. #06102, 9" bear, standing, issue price $8.00
1998. #06101, 11" bear, sitting, issue price $11.00 each,
1998. #06103, 11" bear, standing, issue price $11.00

Same description for all four bears: brown plush body, beige muzzle, black plastic nose, denim style cuffed removable pants, single side seam stitch. Brown leatherette belt with "Smokey" in black on belt with yellow leatherette border, tan hat with "Smokey" on front, brown leatherette hat band, stitched paws and feet, beige soles, glass eyes surrounded by tan and black color felt.

Difference in the soles of the bear's feet. The standing bears have flat cardboard feet covered by short nap plush material, medium brown in color. The sitting bears have beige long nap plush soles.

There are two manufacturer's tags on the bears located on the back of the pants. (1) "Smokey Collection" "Wild Wonders by Northern Gifts." (2) Generic "Northern Gifts" product tag in three languages: English, French, and German. Hangtags are attached at the left ear.

Advertising sheet for Northern Gifts Inc. licensed Smokey bears. Left bottom is #06103, 11" standing Smokey, bottom right is #06102, 9" standing Smokey, top right is #06101, 11" seated Smokey, top right is #06100, 9" seated Smokey.

L.L. Knickerbocker Co., 1998

In 1998, the L. L. Knickerbocker Company, located in Rancho Santa Margarita, California, had Penny Noble design a Smokey Bear for them in celebration of their 75th anniversary. The bears, a limited edition of 5,000, were manufactured in China. The 18" bear came in a muslin bag with nap raiser, bear care guide, and owner's registration card.

1998. PA-1732, 18" poseable bear, jointed arms and legs, brown cotton plush body and feet, removable denim style jeans with red hankie in back pocket, tan faux leather belt, faux leather belt buckle with "Smokey" in bold tan letters,. Black shoe-button safety eyes, black hand-stitched nose, open pink felt mouth, brown felt paws with black stitching, tan muzzle. No name on tan hat with brown ribbon hat band. Hangtag is a metal disk sewn to left breast (like a badge) with Knickerbocker , bear name, and logo. Manufacturer's tags (3) located in back at belt line. (1) Knickerbocker Bear Co. (recycle fiber fill), (2) "New Generation Collection" "Smokey", with the number of the edition "XXX of 5,000" (3) Generic tag with material content. 1999 retail catalog price $76.

Smokey by L. L. Knickerbocker, shown here in a catalog advertisement - 18" from paw to hat, jointed, limited edition, in jeans, belt and hat. No badge. Comes in a Knickerbocker collector's pouch with Bear Care Guide booklet, fur brush, and official registration. 1999 Catalog price: $76.

Cooperstown Bears, 1999

Cooperstown Bears is located in Buffalo Grove, Illinois. They have been in the business of making high quality bears (beginning with uniformed baseball team bears) since 1993.

1999. 16", 100% mohair, designed by Beverly White, officially licensed by U.S.F.S, limited edition of 888 pieces worldwide. The brown bear with tan muzzle, black nose, amber eyes, and black stitched mouth, stitched paws and toes, wears cuffed blue denim jeans with belt loops, a black belt with brass-like buckle which says "SMOKEY." He carries a wooden handled shovel and a tin pail. His light beige hat has a dark brown slender band and "SMOKEY" above it in cinnamon brown lettering. He wears no badge. Retail price $295.00. (This listing added by the author.)

April 1999 magazine advertisement introducing Cooperstown Bears new 16", 100% mohair, licensed Smokey Bear interpreted by Beverly White, limited edition of 888 pieces. Smokey wears cuffed jeans, a belt, beige hat, and carries a metal pail and wooden handled shovel.

Smokey Bear Hand Puppets

Compiled by Fire Captain Richard C. Yokley

Ideal Toy Company

1962. 9" tall, 5-1/2" wide (paw to paw), rubber head attached to cloth Smokey body of brown chest and denim pants, with shovel and Ranger badge all silk screened onto yellow cloth. Back of Smokey's head incised: "Ideal Toy Corp." Original packing label: "Smokey the Bear Hand Puppet, Made in USA 1962, Ideal Toy Corp."

1965. 8-3/4" tall, 8" wide (paw to paw), vinyl head 4-1/4" tall, with a brown plush body 4-1/2" long from base of neck to where body attaches to the head with brown bias tape ties. No paws. Back of head incised: "© 1965 IDEAL TOY CORP., SB-M 216."

1969. Same description as above. Head incised: "© 1969 IDEAL TOY CORP., SB-H 155"

J.J. Wind

1995. 12" tall, brown plush body, beige muzzle, open mouth, plastic nose, light brown stiff felt hat, hangtag left ear, manufacturer's tag left side of neck. Manufactured in China by "Bejing Ssoraso Carmet & Toy Co." Issue price $17.45.

1998. 6" finger puppet, dark brown body and feet, beige muzzle, pink open mouth, plastic nose, denim style pants, metal buckle on brown leatherette belt.

Introduced in 1995, a 12" plush J.J. Wind Smokey Bear hand puppet wearing his "Smokey" hat. Issue price was $17.45. *Photo courtesy of Michael Kruckenberg.*

Inflatable Smokey

Compiled by Fire Captain Richard C. Yokley

Ideal Toy Co.

Date Unknown. 14" "Roly Poly" style, all vinyl, no legs or feet, sand or similar material in base (bear's bottom) to keep bear upright.

Date Unknown. 14" sitting style with legs and feet

Both bears are brown with yellow muzzle, paws and feet. They are dressed in blue pants. The yellow hat and belt buckle have "Smokey" spelled out in brown. The badge says: "Prevent Forest Fires."

Play Pal Plastics

1972. "Roly Poly" style, size and description unknown.

Jennie G. Sales Co.

Mid-1970s. 24" and 54" Smokey figure, full body standing, brown body, blue pants, yellow muzzle, yellow hat and yellow belt buckle, both with "Smokey" in brown, no badge, red shovel with "Prevent Forest Fires" on blade of shovel. Original price for 24" bear $1.98, original price for 54" unknown..

Mid-1970s. 32" PUNCHING BAG, blow up with sand weighted bottom, standing Smokey with both paws holding on to end of shovel with red blade pointing down. Says, "Prevent Forest Fires" beneath standing Smokey on a white background.

Unknown Manufacturer

1970s. A Smokey Bear CHAIR. Two section blowup. When both sections are filled, Smokey's head becomes the back of the chair. His arms/paws become the arms of the chair. His lower body forms the seat of the chair. No badge. When child is sitting in the chair it gives the appearance that the child is sitting in Smokey's lap and is being hugged by Smokey. Exact dimensions are unknown. Possibly a Jennie G. Sales product as its facial features and coloring are similar to her other inflatables.

Date Unknown. BEACH BALL with various photos of Smokey and bear cubs.

"Friends of Smokey Bear" Balloon

86 feet high, head and hat only, head diameter is 55 feet, nose is 10 feet long, eye width is 8 feet, and hat brim is 70 feet. Weighs 525 pounds without basket, holds 120,000 cubic feet of hot air. Made with 4,670 square yards of material and sewn together with five miles of thread, designed and made by the Aerostar balloon company in Sioux Falls, South Dakota. First flight was October 2, 1993.

Macy's Thanksgiving Day Parade Balloon

Full body, 59 feet tall, helium filled. First parade appearance was in 1966. No other information available.

Advertising Smokey

The manufacturers listed below have combined with the U.S. Forest Service and/or the Ad Council in the promotion of Smokey Bear and fire prevention. The promotion involved either the actual sale or use of a Smokey item or the purchase of a product to get a Smokey free or at a discount. Entries are arranged by date, manufacturer/product, Smokey item.

1950s. Kellogg's Cereal Co. - Smokey Bear mask on back of Rice Krispies cereal box

1950s. Smokey Animal Cookies - packed for Saddle Rock Products, Inc., Flushing, NY by Federal Sweets and Biscuit Co., Inc., Chiften, NJ (added by author)

1952. Caterpillar Trucks - Magazine print ad

1957. Nabisco Shredded Wheat - Smokey Bear insert card promoting fire prevention

1960s. Coca-Cola - Posters with Smokey and Coke

1965. Colgate Palmolive Co. - 9-1/2" tall plastic figure of Smokey containing "Soakie" soap

late1960s. Timberland Products Co. - Smokey's image used on lump charcoal, lighter fluid, Bar-B-Ques hickory chips, and briquettes.

1970s. Husky Industries - Same product line as Timberland with the addition of Smokey's image used on fireplace logs and instant lighting charcoal

1970s. Timberline Inc. - Smokey Bear beef jerky and beef teriyaki sticks, and Smokey Bear Original Beef Sausage.

1971/73. Planters Peanuts - Smokey Bear and Mr. Peanut coloring book.

1967 & 1976. Lever Brothers "Aim Toothpaste" - 8" vinyl Smokey by R. Dakin, original price $1.00 and one "net weight statement" from any Aim carton (1972 date also attributed to this item) (Unknown if coincidence but 1976 is the year the original Smokey Bear died at the National Zoo, Washington DC.)

1960s & '70s. Snap-Tab Litterbag Co - Paper litterbags with Smokey's image, with an area for advertising imprint such as Sears, banks, etc.

1978. "Bic" Corporation Cigarette Lighter (withdrawn from distribution) - Smokey poster admonishing you to "Flick Your 'Bic' Carefully in My Woods."

1979. Winchell's Donut House - Smokey urging help to reforest burned out areas

1980s. Great American Service Merchandising - Great American Solar Bar-B-Q, image of Smokey and two cubs on the item

1983. Jameson Home Products "Code One Smoke Detector" - 12" plush Smokey by R. Dakin

1985. McCulloch Chainsaws - Smokey on fire prevention stickers and posters urging careful use of the tool, and

1990 Advertisement for obtaining 12" sitting Three Bears Smokey from Johnson & Johnson for $14 and 5 proofs of purchase of Band-Aid products. *Courtesy of Fire Captain Richard Yokley.*

that "spark arrester screens and muffler guards be used on all portable outdoor power equipment."

1985. Timberline Quality Confections - Smokey Bear gummi candies

1985. Johnson & Johnson - 8" brown hard plastic Smokey (looks like R. Dakin Smokey) - Cost 5 proofs of purchase from Johnson & Johnson products

1988. Naugles/Del Taco (Mexican fast food outlet) - Children' s meal box with Smokey and fire prevention tips.

1990s. American Camper - Smokey's image on various camping gear products

1990. Johnson & Johnson - 12" Smokey Bear, sitting, by Three Bears Co. (obtained with sales slips for Band-Aid products) Cost $14 and 5 proofs of purchase, 40 cents off coupon expired 5/31/90

1994. Mrs. Fields Cookies - "Happy 50th Anniversary" sticker on cookie bags (distributed Washington, D.C. only at 50th Anniversary celebration on the Mall)

1994. Swiss Dairy (Riverside, California) - 50th Anniversary poster on a milk carton

1998. Subaru Motor Company (promoting Subaru's new SUV "Forester") - Smokey Bear, in costume at car shows, handing out fire prevention materials

1998. North American Baking Cookies and Crackers licensed to produce "Smokey Bear and Friends Animal Crackers" but not yet seen..

Information courtesy of Fire Captain Richard C. Yokley, © 1999.

Certificate from Winchell's Donut House for planting a tree to help with reforestation, 1979. *Courtesy of Fire Captain Richard Yokley.*

Smokey Miscellaneous

Because Smokey has been around for more than fifty years, the different items bearing his likeness number in the hundreds, maybe thousands. You'll find Smokey's image on badges, bookmarks, rulers, hats, shirts, backpacks, lunch boxes, bike bottles, glasses and mugs, bibs, stickers, jewelry, stationery, aprons, miniature trucks, knife handles, license plate holders, spoon and bell handles, belt buckles, banks, desk sets, sun visors, watches and alarm clocks. As well as on shoe laces, collector plates, cookie cutters, cookie jars, salt and pepper shakers, flashlights, wallets, posters, playing cards, key chains, blankets, waste baskets, tissue and soap dispensers, place mats, commemorative coins, calendars, greeting cards, tote bags, trash bags, Frisbees, kites, and mouse pads, just to name a few. Many items were offered only during 1994 to commemorate Smokey's 50th birthday. The Smokey Bear Collection figurines and music boxes by Lefton, and miniature Little Smokey figurines by the Hamilton Collection are delightful and bring Smokey to life in endearing poses.

Above: A Washington State University extension forester traveling and working in eastern Russia discovered the region's famous *matryoshka* or nesting dolls. With Smokey and his forest friends in mind, the forester obtained permission from the USDA Forest Service. Woodland Enterprises assisted in the venture, and their catalog got an exclusive on the 5 piece handcrafted, individually painted little works of art. They were introduced in 1996, at the extremely reasonable price of $35 per set. They are no longer available. *Photo courtesy of Michael Kruckenberg.*

Right: 4" handpainted figurine titled "Time to Plant, " shown here on the Woodland Catalog cover. A kneeling little Smokey holds shovel and a small tree. His forest friends look on in approval. Catalog price: $18 plus shipping.

An authorized 4-1/2" handpainted figurine of "Little Smokey" called "Friendship Lifts the Heart" is the first of a series to be issued by The Hamilton Collection. It became available in October 1998 at an issue price of $21.43, including shipping but not state taxes.

3-1/2" ceramic single salt or pepper shaker from a set of two, circa 1960s, $25 pair. *Author's collection.*

14" molded, painted hard plastic bank. Coins go in a slot on top of the "Prevent Forest Fires!" sign. Sign is a paper sticker on molded plastic. Marking on back: "© Play Pal Plastics, Smokey the Bear, 1972." $15-$55.

Junior Forest Ranger's Kit - The 24 page *Junior Forest Ranger Handbook* is © 1987 USDA Forest Service. The remainder of the kit, from 1994, includes a blue letter from Smokey signed with his paw print, a blue membership card, decal, a blue rectangular sign to put in your window saying "I pledged to prevent forest fires!" And the item the children no doubt liked best, a white plastic pin-on badge with the words: "Only You Can Prevent Forest Fires, Junior Forest Ranger" and Smokey's hat and head within a circle. The kit was free by written request. *Author's collection.*

3-1/2" milk glass mug with a smiling Smokey Bear drawn in brown along with "Help prevent forest fires." $10-$35.

The reverse of Smokey milk glass mug has a brown drawing of Smokey Bear pouring water on a campfire while another little bear shovels the ashes. Undated, unmarked.

Smokey Bear hats for a child and an adult. Paper tag on adult hat: "3 West Corp/Official licensee/Cooperative Forest Fire Prevention Program/San Diego." Tag on child's hat: "C53, © 3 West Corp. 1983." *Courtesy of John & Shelley DeWitt, photo by Robert C. McDonald, Sr.*

Smokey Bear Sign - Smokey figure checking out the fire index in Muskegon, Michigan, 1990.

Chapter 2
Storybook Spokesbears

Some bears we can picture in our mind's eye the minute we hear their names. Baloo, Berenstain, Care Bears, Paddington, Pooh, and Yogi are a few of these. They have all been featured in advertising campaigns to sell scores of products, usually unrelated to their storybook *persona*. Their instant name recognition and readymade audience are attributes that make them perfect spokesbears. Most of these bears have had nonfiction books written about them. To learn more about the bears' character and adventures, read their storybooks. For your edification and enjoyment, here are thumbnail sketches and little known facts on each of the storybook spokesbears (and their creators) included in this book.

13" Papa Berenstain Bear by Fisher Price, 1982, dressed in an attached yellow and black plaid shirt, blue overalls, and brown hat. #778 (size is also given as 14-3/4"). Note that the box is cream colored and he is facing left. Original price at February 1982 Toy Fair: $7.95 each. Current MIB: $75-$95 each. *Courtesy of Sandy and Clark McKenzie.*

Berenstain Bears

Philadelphia artists/writers Stanley and Janice (Stan and Jan) Berenstain (now 75) created the Berenstain Bears — Mama, Papa, Brother, and Sister — more than 30 years and 100 book titles ago. Theodor Geisel, better known as Dr. Seuss, was the Berenstain's editor for 17 years. In 1996 their books were deemed the biggest sellers in publishing history at 167 million sold in the United States. They have been translated into 14 languages. With a fan base like that, of course, the Berenstain Bears have been persuaded to advertise or endorse numerous products. Plush toys, games, videos, chocolates, clothes, and a 12 acre theme attraction at Cedar Point Amusement Park in Sandusky, Ohio, plus two other theme parks, to name a few. Of special interest to bear collectors are the stuffed bears made by Knickerbocker, Fisher-Price, Chosun, Emotions (Mattel), and Ace Novelty.

Fisher Price, 1982, 13" Papa Berenstain (#778) and 12" Mama Berenstain (#779) (Assortment, 3 of each, #777).Mama came clad in a blue dress and dust cap with white polka dots. Her flowered panties are part of her body. Note reddish-orange box, and Papa is facing right. Original price: $7.95 each. Fisher Price produced them for that one year only. Current MIB: $75-$95 each. *Courtesy of Sandy and Clark McKenzie.*

Papa and Mama Berenstain , Fisher Price 1982, with 9" Brother Berenstain (#780) seated showing the box backs. It is believed that Sister Berenstain is #781. Fisher-Price tags "© 1962, 1982 S & J Berenstain, Assembled in Mexico." All came in open front display boxes. (Both bear and Fisher Price toy collectors vie for these.) MIB: $75-$95 each. *Courtesy of Sandy and Clark McKenzie.*

Fisher Price tush tags #778, #780, from Papa and Brother, and #779 attached to Mama Berenstain's flowered panties.

10-1/2" standing Sister Berenstain Bear, light golden brown plush, applied ears, up-tilted black plastic nose, plastic eyes, open mouth lined with black felt, pink hair bow, removable pink and white polka dotted blouse, and fully gathered red pants edged with white lace, beige felt-like body, legs and footpads. Ankle tag: "Emotions, A Division of Mattel Toys, Hawthorne, CA, Made in Korea., © 1984 S & J Berenstain." It's likely the other Berenstain bears were made by this manufacturer. $15-$25.

8" seated Sister Berenstain Bear by Knickerbocker. Pink ribbon sewn to rust colored hair which stands on end. Applied ears, black plastic bulb nose, floss mouth, plastic eyes (one side glancing), beige felt foot soles. Pink waffle-weave cotton overalls and white/pink print blouse are part of her body. Side tag: "The Berenstain Bears ™// © 1987 S and J Berenstain." Tag reverse: "ktc//knickerbocker// KNICKERBOCKER TOY CO.// Middlesex , NJ// Surface washable//Sewn in San Pedro, Dom Rep." Probably the other three Berenstain bears were also made by Knickerbocker. $35-$50.

Sister Berenstain, 17" standing, golden beige plush and paws. Her hot pink cotton overalls and polka dotted blouse are part of her body. Plastic eyes, black velour nose, floss mouth. Leg tag: "The Berenstain Bears™//Sister Bear®//© 1993 S&J Berenstain//Mfg & Distr.//By Chosen Int'l Inc." Tag reverse: "Made in P.R. China." Very soft and huggable. $25. *Courtesy of Peggy Monahan.*

A pair of 8" soft stuffed Brother Berenstain plush bears. They appear to be alike, but they are tagged differently. The bear on the left's tag on his back seam reads: "GT Publishing Corp, New York, NY,10016, Made in China." The bear on the right's leg tag says: "The Berenstain Bears™, Brother Bear ®, © 1993 S & J Berenstain, Mfg & Distr. By Chosun Int'l Inc." Tag reverse: "© Chosun International Inc, Made in P.R. China." Paper ear tag pictures the Berenstain Bear family, says "© 1993 S & J Berenstain, Mfg & Distr by Chosun Int'l Inc." Paper tag reverse: washing instructions, "Marketed by WAL-MART Stores, Inc., Bentonville, Arkansas, Tag printed in Hong Kong, Content Made in China." Original Wal-Mart sales ticket on bear on the right reads "$5.97." A bear specialty shop in February 1994 priced the Chosun Brother at $19.95; Sister: $18.95; Mama: $31.50; Papa: $31.95.

Two solidly stuffed Papa Berenstain Bears. The 11" standing Papa in yellow hat has lost his tag. The 8" Papa with brown hat has a foot tag: "Ace Novelty Co. Inc." Tag reverse: "Berenstain Bears, © 1989 S&J Berenstain, Ace Novelty Co Inc, authorized licensee, Made in China." Both Papas have chubby tummies, and applied ears. Papa with tag: $18-$30; without tag: $10-$15.

13" (standing) Papa Berenstain of golden brown plush has plastic eyes and velour nose. Blue cotton overalls and yellow plaid shirt are part of his body. Overalls "buttons" are felt circles sewn on; stuffed flannel-like hat has orange cotton band and is stitched to his head. Tush tag: "All new materials, stuffed with polyester fiber…GT Publishing Corp, New York, NY 10018// Made in China." $20-$35.

"The Berenstain Bears Go to the Movies" book and plush Papa Bear boxed gift set, " © 1997 Family Time Books, Inchworm Press, an imprint of GT Publishing Corporation, Made in China." Box is 8-1/2" tall. Original toy store price: $10.

"The Berenstain Bears Go Out to Eat" book and plush Mama Bear boxed gift set, "© 1997 Family Time Books, Inchworm Press, an imprint of GT Publishing Corporation, Made in China." Box is 8-1/2" tall. Original toy store price: $10.

13" light brown Mama Berenstain has plush head with applied ears and shaggy hair, plush arms and foot-tops. Her body is light blue flannel; foot-soles are beige flannel. Oval plastic eyes are up-looking, black plastic nose is the size of an olive. Eyebrows and wide mouth are black floss. Her removable blue and white polka dot cotton dress fastens with Velcro® in the back, and is trimmed at neckline and hemline with white scalloped eyelet. She carries a woven basket with tiny lavender silk flowers. A pair of matching flowers trims her yellow cotton hat, whose brim is surrounded with red bias tape. A plastic hand tag says: "E, Emotions ™" in blue script. A woven leg tag reads "Emotions...© 1984 S&J Berenstain." Tag reverse reads: "A Division of Mattel Toys/Hawthorne Calif 90250/Made in Korea." $20-$35.

8" handmade Mama Berenstain Bear has tan felt head, hands, and shoes. Red velvet top and legs form her body; removable striped cotton skirt, black bead eyes, built up nose, applied felt ears, wears white velvet dust cap with lace edge and red ribbon trim. No tags. $7-$12.

Miniature McDonald figures from 1986 with their original accessories, except for Sister's horse. Figures: $3-$6 each; accessories: $3-$6 each.

Three sizes of Mama Berenstain bears. The smallest (8") Mama's dress is non-removable because the sleeves are part of her arms. She is most likely missing her dust cap. "Ace" foot tag is dated © 1989 and matches 8" Papa Bear's. The 10" Mama has a not easily removable dress, a sewn on dust cap, and a white "Ace" tag "© 1989, Made in Thailand." The 11-1/2" Mama has a blue "Ace" tag "© 1989, Made in China." All have applied ears. $12-$25 each with tags.

The Berenstain Bears' Life with Papa © 1990, was part of a set of 4 books (*The Berenstain Bears and the Attic Treasure, The Berenstain Bears, and the Substitute Teacher,* and *The Berenstain Bears and the Eager Beavers*) sold at McDonald's to encourage kids to read. Inside book's back cover: "Be sure your children have their own library cards. Your librarian is an excellent source for choosing stories. Brought to you by McDonald's in cooperation with the American Library Association." The 2-1/2" x 3" plastic teeter-totter, photo center, is marked on the bottom: "© 1994 S&J Berenstain, China." The figures, 4" Papa, 3-1/2" Mama, 3" Brother, and 2-1/2" seated Sister are marked "© 1986 S&J Berenstain, China." It would appear that at least 3 times the Berenstain Bears were used in McDonald's promotions. Single book: $1-$3; set of 4 books: $10-$12; figures: $3-$6 each.

The back of the "Life with Papa" book listing the four books in the series.

Set of miniature Berenstain family plush bears with metal keychain holders attached to the backs of their heads. Papa is 6-1/2" from hat to foot, Mama is 5-1/2", Brother 5", and Sister 4-1/2". Their cotton clothes are part of their bodies. Tush tag reads: "The Berenstain Bears ™" and the name of the individual bear "Papa Bear," "Mama Bear," "Brother Bear," or "Sister Bear." Then "© 1997 S&J Berenstain// Mfg & Distr//By Chosun Intl, Inc." Tag reverse says: "Made in China." Paper tag on keychain says: "KEYZ" Original discount store price: $16 per set.

Just two of the numerous Berenstain Bears products on the market, washable marking pens and a card game. Card game "© 1991, 1983 by Berenstain Enterprises Inc, Berenstain Bears is a registered trademark of Stanley and Janice Berenstain. All other trademarks are the property of Western Publishing Company Inc. Produced in U.S.A. by Western Publishing Company, Inc., Racine, Wisconsin." Markers in box: $3-$5; card game (all 40 cards): $6-$10.

Paddington Bear

Can you believe it? Paddington Bear celebrated his 40th birthday in 1998. (Eden issued a special 13" plush Paddington with "40th Anniversary Edition" in script on his navy blue duffel coat.) The waif bear — found sitting on his suitcase in front of the lost and found department, wearing a sign, "Please take care of this bear. Thank you." — was created by author and former BBC cameraman, Michael Bond. The chance purchase of a forlorn looking bear hand puppet and the proximity of Paddington Station stimulated Mr. Bond's imagination and Paddington Bear was the happy result. Paddington titles number "around 70." The storybooks have been translated into 20 languages for worldwide distribution (estimated at 30 million). In 1992 Paddington starred in his own television cartoon series, seen in most English speaking countries plus France, Greece, Germany, and Holland. He has also appeared in a comic strip, musical play, radio shows, and as a Macy's Thanksgiving Parade balloon. A rock band and race horse were named for him. His replica stands in a glass case at the real Paddington Station in London. A Paddington bear was the first item passed through the completed Channel Tunnel by British tunnelers. Paddington accompanied Prime Minister Thatcher to a Conservative Party conference, represented the American Red Cross, and was UNICEF's Friendship Ambassador to Japan. Japan has several specialty stores selling items related to this marmalade loving bear. And Karen, daughter of Paddington's creator, had (in 1992) a London shop devoted to Paddington Bear memorabilia.

Although most Paddington Bears will be found in duffel coat, felt hat, and Wellington (rain) boots, other outfits like monogrammed sweaters, running suit, tuxedo, chef's hat and apron, and raincoat were made for him for the American market (licensee Eden Toys). Both British and American distributors dressed him in rugby gear. (Paddington's Peruvian Aunt Lucy was also manufactured as a stuffed bear but is extremely difficult to find.) The original designer— Shirley Gabrielle Clarkson of Gabrielle Designs in Yorkshire, England, after 25 years of production — filed for bankruptcy in February 1998. Her Paddington Bears were handcrafted in rural Yorkshire entirely of British materials.

In addition to books and stuffed bears, Paddington' s name and likeness can be found on more than 350 varied products, including children's school supplies, notebooks, stationery, stickers, carrying cases, coffee mugs, T-shirts, games, puzzles, pajamas and other clothing, bedding, wallpaper, candy molds, marmalade, Christmas ornaments, and thimbles. A new HBO Paddington television series is planned.

Paddington's Aunt Lucy from Darkest Peru. A very hard-to-find bear. Note her glasses and *babushka* under her black felt hat. She wears a white trimmed red cape and a multi-patterned skirt. Her paper tag says: "Paddington Bear's Aunt Lucy." She carries a shopping bag circa 1987 with Paddington's picture on it. *Courtesy of George B. Black, Jr., Teddy Bear Museum of Naples, Florida.*

A real advertising bear - 15" standing, soft beige plush Paddington Bear dressed in yellow felt hat, red felt duffel coat with toggle buttons, and a "Craftsman ®" tools denim apron with a pocket for his soft stuffed hammer. No boots. On the reverse of his "Please look after this Bear, Thank You!" tag it says: "Darkest Peru to London, England, via Paddington ® Stn, Paddington ® Bear, Kids Gifts ®, Made in China, Tag printed in Hong Kong." His paper tag reads: "Kids Gifts ®, Paddington Bear, Craftsman ®," and shows him using his hammer. On the back of his paper tag: "Kids Gifts, Jersey City, NJ" and "Authorized Representative, Eden International Ltd, London, England." Christmas 1997, original price: $19.99.

Holiday Paddington Bear (15" standing) with ornament included. He's dressed for the festivities in a deep green felt hat and red felt coat with green and yellow felt closures. He carries his own little shopping bag which holds a green ornament with his picture on it. Same information on paper tag backs as "Craftsman" Paddington. Front of paper tag and shopping bag show Paddington standing next to a lighted Christmas tree. Leg tag: "Kids Gifts, Paddington & Co Ltd,, Sears, Made in China." Date on bottom of shopping bag "© P & Co, Ltd 1997." Christmas 1997, original price: $19.99.

For Christmas 1996, Paddington's holiday outfit consisted of a red felt hat, dark green duffel coat with red felt closures. No boots.

A trio of 10" Paddingtons all set to root for their team. The bear in hooded duffel coat and yellow hat is bundled up in case it turns cold. Note he has only one plain toggle-type button fastened with a felt loop. The two in knitted sweaters hold white plastic "bull horns" to make their cheers more audible. They have identical woven leg tags: "© Eden Toys Inc, 1975, 1981, New York, NY, USA, Produced in Korea under license of Paddington and Co. Ltd, London, England." In 1996 for a 2 day sale in November Sears offered a 10" Paddington in yellow hat and blue coat free with any "$40 purchase of kids' apparel." Bears: $20-$35 each.

At a Veteran's Day sale, 1995, Paddington sported a Sears exclusive outfit of red felt hat, red and green sweatshirt with "PB" in white, and a white felt star ornament with his face in a circle on the star's center. The sale price was $13.99.

5" jointed plush Paddington dressed for soccer in a red felt hat, white shorts, navy blue shirt that says "P.B. Club" His red and white soccer sox are plastic atop his black shoes. Of course he wears his "Please look after this bear. Thank You" tag. His tiny shirt tag reads: "© 1987, Eden Toys Inc H/B, Made in Korea." The clear plastic shopping bag he's in would make it easy to hang him on your holiday tree. The bottom of the bag says "© 1990." *Courtesy of Lavonne Morrell.*

Everybody knows it rains a lot in England. In 1993 an 11" "Rainslicker Paddington" came dressed for inclement weather in a yellow slicker with blue corduroy collar and cuffs, a red "brolly" (or "bumbershoot") and of course, his black Wellington boots. Issue price: $24.00.

14" solidly stuffed (not bendable) standing Paddington bear, beige all plush with black ears and dark brown footpads, plastic eyes, brown floss nose, in yellow rain slicker with his initials "P.B." machine embroidered in red on the chest. Slicker has mandarin collar and fastens with two brass-like snaps. A mark at his ankles indicates he's probably missing his Wellington boots. His rain hat is also gone. It is not known if he came with an umbrella. His woven leg tag reads: "Copyright © Eden Toys Inc., 1972, 1981, produced in Korea under license..." Without hat and boots: $10-$15; with hat, boots, and umbrella: $25-$35.

13" standing Paddington dressed in removable red nightshirt, nightcap and slippers. Nightcap and slippers are tacked on. Slippers have knobby white plastic soles. Three red plastic buttons on the navy blue neck placket of the nightshirt. A white painted paw print on the nightshirt chest. The plush of this beige bear is especially silky. Plastic eyes and nose, floss mouth. Woven leg tag front: Washing instructions and "eden®" Tag reverse: "© Eden Toys Inc., NY, NY, Made in Indonesia." No dates given. $25-$40.

September 1995 brought wardrobe options to some 12" Paddingtons - an artist in beret and splash apron holding a brush and palette, a traveler with suitcase and passport in hand, and a shopper with a bag from "Bearingtons." Issue price (including bear) was $25 each from Eden Toys.

The fourth 1995 wardrobe option for 12" plush Paddington was a magician's outfit seen in this Eden Toys advertisement. It is complete with black pants, white shirt, red tie, black cape, and of course, a rabbit. Issue price (included bear): $25 from Eden Toys.

These plush Paddingtons are nearly the same size. Bear in blue duffel coat is 15" standing, and bear in blue sweatshirt is an inch shorter. Note that the coat is a double-breasted style with 4 plain plastic toggle buttons fastened with felt loops. Their leg tags are the same "© Eden Toys 1975, 1981." Note their dark brown footpads. $20-$30 each.

An 8" seated beige plush Paddington in blue felt hat and red felt hooded duffel coat. Note the two grooved plastic toggle buttons fastened with cord coming from leatherette triangles. No boots. Woven leg tag is a fairly recent one. Washing instructions and "© Kids Gifts™" on tag front and "SEARS, Made in Indonesia" on the reverse. $10-$15.

A trio of tiny Paddingtons. The 5" red coated plush bear is jointed, and can stand alone in his black plastic Wellington boots Red hatted 3-1/2" Paddington, center, has paws that clip on. They each have tags on their coat hems. Red coat © 1986 and clip on © 1985. Smallest Paddington (2-1/2") is dressed in glued-on flannel pajamas, red hat, and carries his suitcase. Paper sticker tag on his foot says "H.C.F., Made in Hong Kong." 5": $8-$15; 3-1/2": $6-$12; 2-1/2": $4-$10.

14" sweatshirt Paddington shows off the message on his back "Please look after this Bear. Thank You."

Shopping Bag Paddington with Video - 5" light beige plush-over-frame Paddington in yellow felt hat, blue velour hooded duffel coat and black plastic Wellington boots. Bottom of bag says: "© 1998" and "Made in China." The 30 minute color video is by Time-Life for Kids, titled "The Adventures of Paddington Bear." The 3 stories included are "Paddington at the Wheel," "Howdy Paddington!," and "A Shopping Expedition." The back of the video box has a 50th anniversary message from author Michael Bond. Retail price including shipping: $40.

A quartet of 10" Paddingtons. Bear second from left in red coat has an underarm tag that reads: "©Eden Toys Inc, NY, NY, Made in Colombia." (The first from this country I've seen.) His face is smaller and thinner and less bear-like than the bears on the right in blue coats. His fur is less soft and less dense than the plush of the blue-coated bears. His footpads are dark brown felt. The far-left bear has no body tag, but otherwise matches his red-coated brother. The blue-coated Paddingtons have leg tags that read: "Eden Toys Inc ©, NY, NY 10001, Made in Korea." Their footpads are brown plush. The paper tags on red and blue coated bears are identical with "© Eden Toys" and the date "1975." All 4 have ears of felt rather than plush. $10-$15 each

Shopping Bag Paddingtons - 5" light brown plush-over-frame bears wearing felt hats, hooded duffel coats, and black plastic Wellington boots. Coat hem tags say: "Eden" and "Made in Korea." The cardboard shopping bag is dated "© 1987." The red coated bear is missing his shopping bag. Bear without bag: $10-$15, bear with bag: $15-$20

Paddington Bear tree ornament "Home for Christmas" (1997) from the Heirloom Collection of Carlton Cards. Issue price: $14.95.

7" velour Paddington bear rattle with floss facial features and paper "Please take care of this bear. Thank you." tag. Woven tag at back neck seam gives washing instructions and reads "eden®", reverse: "©Eden Toys Inc., Made in China." No dates given. $5-$10.

5" rubber squeeze toy Paddington is all one piece. Marked on feet: "© Eden 1976, Hong Kong." Paddington in center has paws that grip (or clip on), wears felt hat, and removable light blue velour coat with hood. Plastic eyes and nose, leatherette footpads. Paper tag: "Please take care of this Bear. Thank You." Cloth tag on coat hem: "© Eden Toys, Inc, Made in Korea." Smallest Paddington (2-1/2") is flocked with a glued-on hooded felt coat. His little suitcase is labeled "Wanted on Voyage." His sticker foot tag says "© Eden, Made in Hong Kong." Rubber bear: $8-$12; clip on: $6-$10; 2-1/2": $4-$6. *Center Paddington courtesy of Peggy Monahan.*

3" Paddington "Bearly Balanced" on skis, "Enesco Treasury of Christmas Ornaments ®, © 1993 Eden Toys, © 1993 Paddington & Co. Ltd., made in China" from Artplas, a moldable poly-material. Issue price: $12.

Top of Paddington decorated tin box, full (4 oz) of bear shaped cookies by Darlington, Fort Wayne, Indiana (on removable paper label) Purchased Christmas 1997. Box itself is not dated or marked. $10.

Figures on side of Paddington tin cookie box help children learn their colors.

Quilted 12" x 9" baby's bib shows Paddington holding a bouquet. No tags. $5-$9.

Handpainted pewter thimble of Paddington ™ Bear strolling across a marmalade jar with suitcase in hand, as shown in 1993 catalog. Catalog 1993 price: $14.95.

On left individual Paddington thank you card, © 1991, on right package of Paddington thank you notes © 1990. Both by Sangamon Inc, Made in USA (Yeh!) Card: $2; notes: $4.

Yogi Bear ®
"Smarter than the Average Bear"

During the 1930s William Hanna and Joseph Barbera quit their office positions and took jobs as cartoonists at MGM Studios. In 1938 this talented pair created the mischievous cat and mouse cartoon characters Tom and Jerry. In 1957, the year they thought up the stone-age Flintstones, Hanna and Barbera formed their own production company. (Flintstone Vitamins have been on the market since 1969!) In 1958 Yogi, BooBoo, Cindy Bear, Huckleberry Hound, and Jellystone Park's Mr. Ranger Smith flowed forth from their creative minds and pens. Later the modernistic Jetsons did likewise.

Yogi Bear was named for the famous baseball player Yogi Berra. More than 3,500 half-hours of animated programming and more than 350 different series, specials, television motion pictures, and films starring Yogi and friends have originated from Hanna-Barbera. Yogi reached star status in 1961 with his own TV series *The Yogi Bear Show* and the release of his own feature film *Hey There, It's Yogi Bear,* in 1964. The Los Angeles 3-acre property where the Flintstones and Yogi Bear were first drawn was denied historic landmark status in 1997 and sold by Time-Warner to Universal Studios.

Almost since his conception Yogi Bear and his friends have been seen in advertisements, on signs, boxes of popcorn and juice, on board games (1980 Milton Bradley), dishes, cups (Arby's), as a premium for French's Mustard (1982, 16" Yogi Bear, $12.99, plus cash register receipt and one "net weight statement"). And of course, in storybooks, coloring books, records, cartoon videos, and as Christmas ornaments. There are currently 70 Yogi Bear's Jellystone Park Camp-Resorts in the United States and three in Canada with resident costumed Yogi and friends to entertain the guests. (Yogi Bear's image is used by permission of Leisure Systems Inc. on behalf of Hanna-Barbera® ©1999.)

Yogi and friends stuffed bears were made by many manufacturers, including: Knickerbocker, Mighty Star, Nanco, Applause, and Hanna-Barbera Productions. In 1996 Cooperstown Bears offered a mohair, boxed set, limited edition of 1,000 (worldwide) of an 8-1/2" BooBoo and a 15-1/2" Yogi holding a picnic basket. The issue price was $295.00. In April 1999 Warner Brothers Studio Store released an 8 inch beanbag Yogi with green porkpie hat and green tie. A beanbag BooBoo made his debut in November 1998. A beanbag Ranger Smith was due for release Summer 1999. No word yet when or whether Cindy Bear, the lovesick southern belle whose heart belongs to Yogi, will join the beanbag line-up.

Yogi's cruising in a Cartoon Network mini-van. *Courtesy of Nancy Kraus, Yogi Bear's Jellystone Park Campground.*

Cartoon Network Yogi - 6" seated Huckleberry Hound is a finger puppet (put two fingers in his arm pockets)© 1996 tag; next to him 7-1/2" seated Yogi and 5" Yogi (finger puppet, second from right) all have the same Cartoon Network tag. In center 9" seated Yogi has Cartoon Club decal on his chest; his tush tag says "Mattel" and "© 1993 Hanna-Barbera Productions." Far right is a velvet bean bag Yogi with a © 1995 tag, "Hanna-Barbera Productions, Christmas Corner, Sun Valley, CA, Made in China." Inside his paper ear tag are facts about Yogi (favorite food, etc.) Only the bean bag has a closed mouth. $6-$15 each.

Advertisement and box of Jolly Time Popcorn shows Yogi enjoying the product. Box is © 1993 and offers a free Cartoon Network "Yogi & Friends" cartoon video ($12.95 value) with 6 proofs of purchase of Jolly Time Popcorn.

Yogi on the box front and individual packet of "Capri Sun All Natural Yogi Berry Fruit Drink" The box is © 1991.

"Yogi Berry" with his friends on the back of the Capri Sun beverage box.

3-3/4" white plastic cups from Arby's show the skating rink antics of Mr. Ranger, BooBoo, Cindy, and Yogi falling through the ice. Marked "© 1993 Hanna-Barbera Productions, Inc." Cups: $4-$6 each.

3-3/4" white plastic cups from Arby's show BooBoo landing in a tree while sledding and Yogi and Cindy cheering him on. Marked "© 1993 Hanna-Barbera Productions" and "© 1993 Arby's Inc." under their logo. Cups: $4-$6 each.

Paper bag from Arby's depicts Yogi, BooBoo, and Quick Draw McGraw enjoying a campfire. *Courtesy of Nancy Kraus, Yogi Bear's Jellystone Park Campground.*

Reverse side of Arby's bag with Yogi giving fire safety tips. *Courtesy of Nancy Kraus.*

A 4-3/4" tall plastic bucket with handle, from Arby's, pictures Huckleberry Hound water skiing. Marked "©1995 Hanna-Barbera Productions, © 1995 Arby's Inc." $2-$4.

On the other side of the bucket, two mice, Pixie and Trixie, are driving the boat, pulling Huckleberry Hound.

A quartet of Hanna-Barbera plush characters currently available at Yogi Bear Campground stores, Yogi 13" and 10", BooBoo 8", Cindy 10", © 1995 Hanna-Barbera Productions. *Courtesy of Nancy Kraus, Yogi Bear's Jellystone Park Campground.*

Some oldie goodie Yogis - On the left is an early 1960s vintage 7-1/2" hollow plastic figure (not a bank or soap bottle). Center of attention goes to an 11" solidly stuffed "Knickerbocker © 1973, sewn in Dominican Republic" with green cotton hat, cotton nose, felt grin and felt eyes. A 9-1/2" slender velvet Yogi by Applause, made in China, with felt hat, felt collar, white ribbon tie, plastic eyes and nose, rounds out the trio. His arms are unstuffed flaps. No date given. Plastic: $7-$15; Knickerbocker: $50-$65; Applause: $20-$35. *From Author's collection.*

These Yogis have lost their tags, but are quite obviously by Mighty Star, circa 1980. 22" standing Yogi: $35; 16" standing Yogi: $25; 11" seated Yogi with collar and tie: $15-$20; 10" seated Yogi without collar or tie, faded hat: $8-$12.

Yogis by Mighty Star © 1980, Left Yogi is 10", center 8", and right 9". The "bookend" bears are both plush, while the center Yogi is felt and has freckles. $15-$25 each.

A group of Yogis and a Huckleberry Hound by Nanco. Yogi in center is 17". Yogis at either side are 11" Huckleberry is 9" and Santa Yogi is 7". All tags say "© 1989" and "Not for retail sale." $8-$20 each.

20" Yogi and 17" Huckleberry Hound cloth cut 'n' stuff pillow dolls. Each has his name printed in large letters on his back. Circa 1970s. $8-$15 each. Dell Comic book Yogi Bear No. 13, July 1963: $5-$15.

Amidst a group of Yogi Bear storybooks sits 10" plush Yogi with freckles whose tag says only "© 1986 Hanna-Barbera Productions." Standing is a softly stuffed 15" Mighty Star Yogi © 1980. He wears a plastic collar and has lost his tie. The 7" tall padded satin tree ornament is by Nanco © 1989 and shows Yogi in the act of kidnapping (or hijacking) a picnic basket. Bears: $10-$20; ornament: $3-$5; books: $1-$6.

15" Huckleberry Hound of flannel-like fabric, felt tie and hat band, with Mighty Star © 1980 tag. He appears to be open mouthed but is not. Huck: $10-$18; books: $1-$6 each.

10" seated blue plush Huckleberry Hound, plastic eyes, side-turned head with straw hat, heavyweight red felt tie and tongue, and "Huck" machine embroidered in red on his right foot. A Hanna-Barbera tag, © 1990. Huck: $15-$20; books: $1-$6.

The lady in Yogi's life, Cindy Bear. 14" tan plush Cindy with pink hair bow, pink ear linings, large plastic eyes and felt eyelashes has "© 1989 Hanna Barbera Productions Inc, Made in China" tag. $15-$20. The 11" greenish gray short plush Cindy wears yellow scarf, aqua felt circle skirt and felt flower on her ear. Tag: "Yogi Bear ™ © 1995, Hanna Barbera Production, Inc, Christmas Corner, Sun Valley, CA, Made in China." She retails currently for $9.95.

Yogi's buddy BooBoo - All 6 BooBoos are plush. All but the 13" bear at far left have eyelids on their plastic eyes. He is the only one with a felt tie. He has a "© 1980 Hanna-Barbera Productions By Mighty Star" "Shell Made in Korea" leg tag. Largest BooBoo is 16" with lavender velour tie and a Nanco "© 1989 Hanna-Barbera Productions Inc, licensed by Hamilton Projects Inc, Country of Origin China, Not for retail sale" tag. The pair of 10" BooBoos on right with "nearly asleep" eyes wear lavender satin ribbon bow ties, have the same tag as 16" Note 10" bear at far right has felt eyebrows; the bear next to him has no eyebrows. Little 8" BooBoo wears flannel-like purple bow tie, back tag reads: "Yogi Bear ™ © 1995, Hanna-Barbera Productions, Inc., All rights reserved, Christmas Corner, Sun Valley, CA, Made in China.". His hair resembles a Mohawk cut, while the 6-1/2" bear's tuft of hair seems more of a cowlick rather than the toupee look of the 4 larger bears. 6-1/2" BooBoo is missing his felt tie and tag. His nose is a little larger than the 8" bear. Book *BooBoo and V.I.V* by Jean Lewis, Illustrated by George DeSantis, © 1965, Whitman Publishing Co., Racine, Wisconsin, Printed in the U.S.A. Book: $5-$10; 16" BooBoo: $10-15; 12-1/2": $15-$18; 10": $6-$10; 6-1/2": $3-$5; 8" currently retails for $6.95.

Small plastic figurines, 3" Yogi, 2" BooBoo, marked on their feet "© 1990 H-B Prod ™, Made in China." Currently retail for $3-$5 each. *Courtesy of Nancy Kraus.*

Yogi Bear beach towel currently for sale at Yogi Bear's Jellystone Campground stores. $6. *Courtesy of Nancy Kraus.*

3-3/4" Hallmark tree ornament, Yogi and BooBoo decorating a picnic basket for Mr. Ranger. *Courtesy of Nancy Kraus, Yogi Bear's Jellystone Park Campground.*

A lying down plush Yogi from the 1960s-1970s large enough for a child to sit on his back. $10-$25.

A 7"x5" "Yo Yogi!"™ magnetic fishing game with Yogi and BooBoo, "© 1991 Hanna-Barbera Productions. " $1-$5.

Shriner, Lt. Colonel (US Army Retired) Jim "Yogi" Kalis of Mt. Vernon, Washington, in his Yogi Bear costume in which he visits children's hospitals and burn units, bringing comforting hugs and cheer. *Photo courtesy of Jeanne Kalis.*

Mealtime Memories - 3-1/2" brown painted plastic Yogi Bear face cup from 1960s, incised mark on bottom: "F.&F. Mold & Die Works Inc, Dayton, Ohio, Made in USA " $8-$15.

7" diameter, circa 1960s, Jellystone Park plate with Yogi and friends getting ready for a party. Raised marking on bottom: "Melmac ®, Dinnerware, 0203-7, Boomton Holding Co, Inc., Boomton, NJ." $6-$10.

Yogi - Ranger Smith is chasing Yogi Bear up a tree for pinching the picnic basket. A really great sign (purchased from an Orlando campground that went out of business) now in use in Arcadia, Florida at Yogi Bear's Jellystone Park Campground. 1998. *Courtesy of Nancy Kraus.*

Yogi - Window display sign at Jellystone Park Campground store, Arcadia, Florida, 1998. *Courtesy of Nancy Kraus.*

Costumed Yogi Bear helps Mr. Ranger Smith control the traffic at Jellystone Park Campground. *Courtesy of Nancy Kraus.*

Yogi Bear figure, bigger than life size, seems to be jogging at Jellystone Park Campground, Arcadia, Florida. *Courtesy of Nancy Kraus.*

Costumed Yogi Bear has "liberated" a picnic basket and BooBoo is pointing out the best place to go to enjoy it. *Courtesy of Nancy Kraus.*

Costumed Yogi Bear holds hands with Cindy Bear statue at Jellystone Park Campground. *Courtesy of Nancy Kraus.*

Winnie the Pooh

To the delight of readers everywhere — and to the disgust of his creator — Winnie the Pooh was an instant literary success. In 1924 A.A.(Alan Alexander) Milne (1882-1956) was a highly respected and successful British mystery writer. He was a member of the Inner Circle, with Agatha Christie, Dorothy Sayers, and other mystery giants of the time. Milne was greatly annoyed to find that the series of stories he wove to amuse his young son Christopher Robin (later also a writer) soon overshadowed his serious novels, plays, and mystery writings. (In the National Portrait Gallery, London, is a photograph taken in 1924 of Milne, Christopher Robin, and the original teddy bear, purchased at Harrods, they called Pooh.) Nearly 75 years after his "birth" Pooh still stirs the hearts and imaginations of a whole new generation of readers and video viewers. And Smokey is not the only bear with his own postage stamp. In 1997 Canada issued a limited edition set of four stamps, one showing a postman and the other three featuring Pooh. Their issue price was $9.95 per sheet of four.

British actor Peter Dennis is the only actor officially authorized to publicly perform Winnie-the-Pooh readings. He first performed his one man show, *Bother!*, in 1976 in honor of the 50th anniversary of the publication of the first Pooh storybook. Since then he has performed *Bother!* over 200 times, including a reading at Westminster Palace.

Nearly any item you can think of has depicted, at one time or another, Winnie-the-Pooh or his friends Piglet, Eeyore, Tigger, Kanga or Roo. Clothes, watches, bedding, curtains, toys, baby items, porch flags, party goods, and hundreds of other products bear Pooh's likeness. One of the best known is probably the Johnson & Johnson plastic figural shampoo bottle (of which there is now a second version). And, of course, the storybooks and millions of stuffed animals.

An early (1940-1956) 12" Pooh with New York address Gund label. Although his tag is a bit frayed, Pooh himself, arched felt eyebrows and all, has survived quite well. Notice his wide-apart foot stance. With him are birthday invitations from Ambassador Cards, a division of Hallmark Cards. Pooh bear: $75-$100; Invitations (8): $3-$5.

California Stuffed Toys Poohs - The 21" seated and 13" seated Poohs in red velour ("Pooh" embroidered) shirts, and the undressed 12" Pooh leaning against big Pooh, have white tags that identify them as "Walt Disney Character." The tag on the 15" Pooh, back row far left, says "Walt Disney Distributing Co., Lake Buena Vista, Florida." The 9" seated baby Pooh wearing red velvet "Pooh" bib also has a "Walt Disney Character" tag. The little 7" baby Pooh (in front) has a beige ribbon tag : "© Walt Disney Productions, Mfg by California Stuffed Toys, Los Angeles." Filled with ground nut shells, he sits like a bean bag. Because these were made in the U.S.A., they probably predate Poohs made overseas (not including England). 21" Pooh: $60-$75; 13" in shirt: $25-$30; undressed Poohs: $10-$15; Poohs with bibs: $12-$18.

A group of Gund/Disney/Sears tagged Poohs. The 14" Poohs with removable red felt shirts and the undressed 12" (working) music box Pooh were "Sewn in Haiti." The 11" seated Pooh on right with removable red sweatshirt, and two 8" seated Poohs, whose shirts are part of their bodies, were "Assembled in Haiti." Circa 1970s. $75-$100 each. Music box Pooh: $80-$100.

These 13" Gund/Disney/Sears tagged Poohs were all "Sewn in El Salvador." Three are plush with velvet or pompom noses and glued-on felt eyebrows. The Pooh second from right is extremely lightweight and not as huggable as the others. He's made from a flannel-like fabric, has a plastic nose and painted on eyebrows, and washing instructions: "Hand wash, line dry." $10-$15 each.

"Made in Republic of Korea" Poohs with stitched eyebrows. All but the 8" seated Pooh in center leaning on the ladder have "Sears/Disney" tags. The 8" Pooh has a woven Gund/Disney/Sears tag. He may be a late Sears/Gund Pooh. The 10" seated Pooh at left is missing his sweater. (Tag says "Remove Sweater and Hand Wash.") The 8" and little 6" seated bears' plush shirts are part of their bodies. Book is a mint condition © 1981 "Golden Sturdy Shape Book." 10" and 6" bears: \$5-\$10; Gund bear: \$10-\$18; book: \$6-\$10.

Sears/Disney/TCA Group Inc. Poohs. The 11" seated "Bedtime Pooh" on the left has a zipper in his back, a good place for treasures or small p.j.s. On the right is 8" seated "Suction Cup Pooh" with side turned head. Right front Pooh measures 5" seated. These 3 are plush and "Made in Korea." The 6" seated Pooh beside "Bedtime Pooh" is a flannelette fabric and was made in China. Fisher-Price storybook is © 1979 and came with a phonograph record (now missing). Bedtime: \$10-\$20; Suction Cup: \$6-\$10; small Poohs: \$3-\$6; book: \$5-\$8.

Some different looking Poohs. The 6" seated Disney/Sears/TCA Group tagged Pooh was made in China and his muzzle is longer and more pointed than the small Poohs made in the Republic of Korea. The 10" seated plush undressed Pooh has a woven Sears/Disney/Gund tag, was made in Indonesia, and is machine washable. It's likely he was one of the last Sears/Gund Poohs made. He's very cuddly. The 4" painted rubber squeak toy is marked on the bottom: "Made in Taiwan, Sold by Sears Roebuck & Co, Chicago, Ill. 60684." The 7" seated peach plush Pooh on the right has glued-on black felt eyes and brows, wears a red velour shirt, and is tagged "Winnie the Pooh, Product of Taiwan, © Walt Disney Productions." He has more of a Piglet look to him. 10": $15-$20; 6": $5-$10; 7": $5-$10; squeak toy: $4-$7.

Although they are untagged, it's not difficult to identify these two Poohs. Because they so closely resemble their relatives, it's safe to say that the 25" Pooh with felt eyebrows on the right was made by Gund. And that the 16" eyebrow-less Pooh on the left came from the California Stuffed Toys factory in Los Angeles. The heavy cardboard wall plaque of Eeyore pulling Pooh in the honey cart is also unmarked and undated, but has a Disney look. 25": $18-$25; 16": $10-$15; plaque: $4-$8.

The 9" plastic (working) musical crib-rail crawler says "Hunny" on Pooh's pot and is marked on the head back: "© Meritus Industries Inc, 1982, Made in Hong Kong, © Walt Disney Productions." On the right the 26" Pooh "Puffet Stuffets™ " is a pillow to hug or lounge with. A pocket under his shirt opens to store pajamas or treasures. It's © Walt Disney and Made in Taiwan. Crawler or Puffet: $8-$15.

15" (when extended) flannel-like Pooh holding a blue honey pot. Floss brows, eyes, nose, and mouth. When he is hung by his head cord and his feet are pulled to their farthest extension, the music box in his head begins to play "Winnie the Pooh." Waist tag: "© Disney, © The First Years Inc., Contents All New Materials, Polyester Fill." Tag reverse: "Do Not Immerse in Water, Surface Wash Only, Made in China." Undated. $15-$20.

The well loved, untagged 10" seated Pooh on the left has plastic eyes, floss nose, and is stuffed with shredded fabric. Possibly he's from the 1950s. The 13" seated bear on the right, a Pooh "wanna-be," has lost his tush tag. The price on these unidentified urchins would be what someone is willing to pay.

Pooh's sidekick Tigger. 14" seated gold and black Tigger (tiger), tag is unreadable but may be California Stuffed Toys "Disney Character" tag. The 6" seated orange Tigger tag says "Sears, Tigger, Walt Disney, Made in the Republic of Korea for Sears Roebuck and Co." Tigger storybook © 1964, 1977 Walt Disney. 14" Tigger: $15-$20; 6" Tigger: $3-$8; book: $1-$5.

Pooh's friend Eeyore - A 6" gray plush donkey with red ribbon on his tail. Tag reads: "Made in Korea, © 1984, A— Novelty Co, Inc., Los Angeles." No mention of Eeyore, Pooh, or Disney so maybe he's a look-alike. $3-$8. Eeyore storybooks: $1-$5.

Pooh's friends Piglet & 'Roo - 6" seated pink plush Piglet, striped suit is part of his body. Tag: "Sears, Piglet ®, Walt Disney, Made in Republic of Korea for Sears." The 9" seated peach plush 'Roo has turquoise ear lining to match his body shirt, black felt eyebrows, and a large brown nose. Tush tag: "Sears, Winnie the Pooh, Walt Disney." Tag reverse: "Assembled in Haiti, Gund Inc,, Edison, NJ." Piglet: $4-$7; 'Roo: $10-$15.

The Easter "Pooh-Gram" included an 11" seated Pooh bear in a fleecy white Easter Bunny suit, and carrying an Easter basket full of jelly beans. Also included were a hard cover storybook "Winnie the Pooh's Easter" and a blank Pooh-Gram card so the giver could write their own message. It was shipped in a box with illustrations of the Hundred Acre Wood, Pooh's House, Tigger's House, and Piglet's House on the four sides. Original price: $29.95 plus tax and shipping (from the Disney Catalog).

Copy of an advertisement for a 1998 Easter "Pooh-Gram."

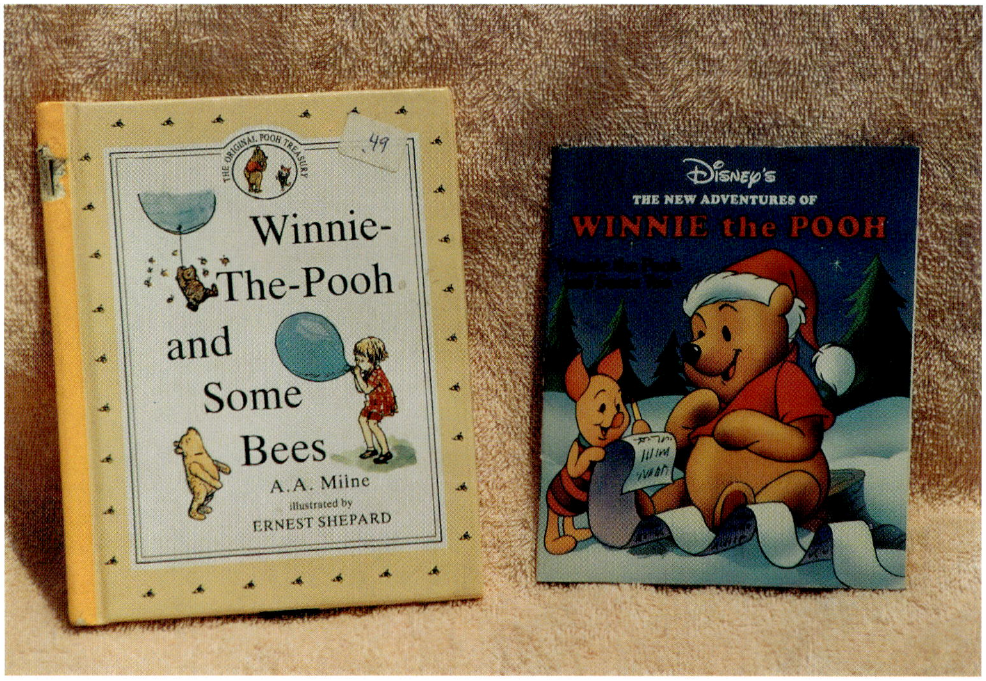

Two Pooh storybooks used as merchandising tools. On the right a 5"x6" hardcover *Winnie the Pooh and Some Bees*, by A.A. Milne, illustrator Ernest Shepard, published by Dutton Children's Books for BP (British Petroleum) in 1990,original price: $4.95. On the right a 4-1/4" x 5" paperback, *Winnie the Pooh and Santa Too*, published by Disney Press for Starburst Fruit Chews, no author or illustrator named, undated. Hardcover: $5-$10; paperback: $2-$5.

Inside covers show the BP and Starburst names. In addition to *Winnie the Pooh and Some Bees* (a single chapter from Milne's original *Winnie-the-Pooh* book), BP sponsored five other chapters as hardcover books: *Pooh Goes Visiting and Pooh and Piglet Nearly Catch a Woozle*, *Piglet Meets a Heffalump*, *Eeyore Has a Birthday*, *Kanga and Baby Roo Come to the Forest*, and *Christopher Robin Gives Pooh a Party*. Disney Press published *Winnie the Pooh's Christmas*.

Since Pooh was "born" over 70 years ago, there has been plenty of time to merchandise him. This advertisement from April 1997 for J.C. Penney's "Baby Days Sale" urges you to "register to win this 48" Pooh® Bear!"

On the left is a bilingual Spanish-English paperback storybook , *The Winnie-the-Pooh Book*, © 1977, 1965, 1964, a Golden Book by Western Publishing Company, Inc. Racine, Wisconsin. On the right is a plastic over cardboard "Turn and Learn" book © 1971 Ideal Toy Corp, Hollis, NY and © Walt Disney Productions. The story is printed inside with dials the child can turn to see pictures corresponding to the numbered paragraphs. Bilingual book: $10-$15; Ideal book: $15-$20.

This K-Mart toy ad from November 1995 gives a choice of Pooh or Eeyore "Read 'N Cuddle" characters with a book. Pooh tree-houses and playsets by Mattel were also suggested.

A "Family Circle" magazine ad states "Pooh makes bedtime friendlier" with a Pooh musical crib-crawler by Mattel.

This magazine ad for Pooh hat and mittens, quotes from a Pooh book "it seemed like an exploring sort of day."

Pooh and friends bottles of Johnson & Johnson products are a familiar Pooh advertising medium.

A Target store ad introduces a new Pooh Johnson & Johnson bottle.

A magazine ad says "It's so much friendlier with Pooh," a new line of apparel, home furnishings, gifts, and toys.

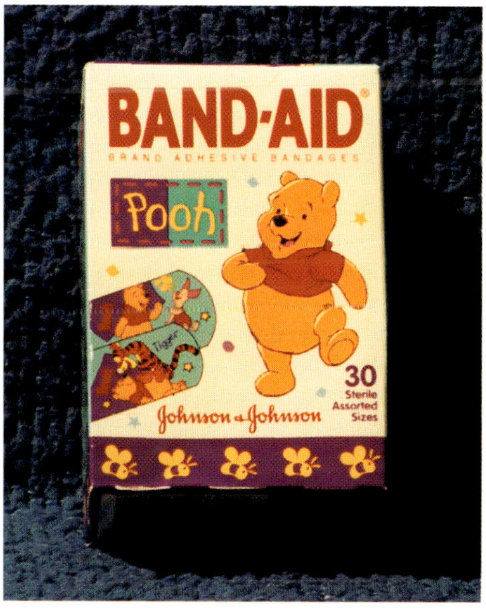

Pooh on the box (front and back) and 30 decorative adhesive bandages inside this Band-Aid® brand box by "Johnson & Johnson Consumer Products Inc., © J&J CPI 1997. Disney material © Disney, based on the Winnie the Pooh works copyright A.A. Milne and E.H. Shepard." Currently available.

A set of five Pooh and friends glasses contained Welch's jams and jellies and advertised (on the glass back) "Only on Video! *Pooh's Grand Adventure*."

A back view of the Welch's Pooh glass set.

Baloo

Baloo is not in the same household word category as Pooh, Paddington, Yogi, and the Berenstains, but as a Disney character he does have his audience. He appeared in *The Jungle Book* and in the *TaleSpin* television and book series. He was used to promote the movie and video, and appeared on the box front of "Carnation Kids Mac-Air-Roni TaleSpin shaped enriched macaroni product." In 1993 Kellogg Company offered 1-1/2" to 2-1/2" "Collector's Edition" vinyl figurines, obtainable for UPC symbols from cereal boxes, plus a small shipping and handling fee. The final four figurines, designated the "Disney Afternoon Tale Spin®" set, included Baloo wearing a pilot's cap, along with Molly, Don Karnage, and Kit.

Grayish brown stuffed plush Baloo bear used to promote the movie and video "The Jungle Book." White snout and paw pads, large brown nose, small plastic eyes with eyebrows, standup fur on head, and chubby tummy. A Wal-Mart newspaper ad of November 1997 showed Baloo and a red/blue star logo saying: "Exclusively © Wal-Mart." Ad caption for the plush animals read: "Baloo and King Louie will be available in Wal-Mart stores this holiday season. Make sure to pick up the home video as well."

In December 1997, a purchase of any 3 Kid Cuisine frozen meals earned a $5 refund on *Disney's Jungle Book* video. Enclosed inside specially marked packages of Kid Cuisine were a series of 8 "Magic Movie Cards" of Baloo and other *Jungle Book* characters.

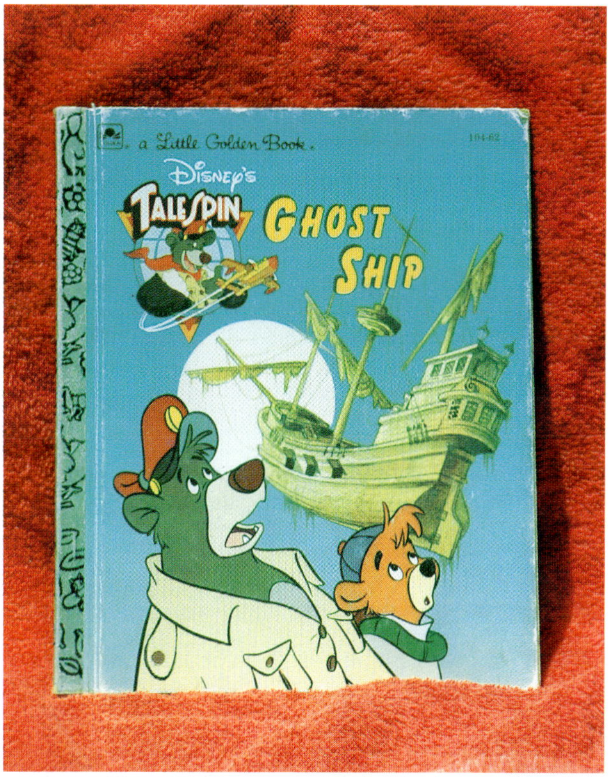

Baloo stars as the hero in *Disney's TaleSpin Ghost Ship* (Little Golden Book, © 1991). His little friend Kit helps. Book near mint condition: $5-$10.

Box front of "Carnation Kids Mac-Air-Roni, TaleSpin Shaped, Enriched Macaroni Product, 14 oz." On the back of the box are TaleSpin finger puppets of Baloo, Kit, and Molly.

4" plastic Baloo seems happy to have discovered a big bunch of bananas. Bottom mark: "Mfg for McD Corp, China Wm Chine, © Disney." (A Golden Arches McDonald's promotion.) On the cover of the paperback *Jungle Book* (© 1967 Golden Book) he relaxes and chats in the jungle. Figure: $3-$9; book: $1-$5.

Care Bears™

In 1982 the American Greetings Corporation conceived the adorable and appealing Care Bears™ and promoted them on greeting cards and a diversity of other items including books, bedding, children's clothes, fabric carrying bags, plastic scissors, metal lunch box and thermos by Aladdin, and vinyl inner tubes for babies, just to name a few. Care Bears were issued in plush, fabric, plastic, ceramic, and wood. Probably the story books and stuffed bears were the most popular of the offerings.

The names of the individual Care Bears ™ are Wish Bear™ (shooting star on tummy), Birthday Bear ™ (cupcake and candle on tummy), Bedtime Bear ™ (crescent moon), Funshine Bear ™ (sun), Love-A-Lot Bear™ (2 hearts), Friend Bear™ (2 flowers), Good Luck Bear ™ (4 leaf clover), Grumpy Bear ™ (rain cloud), Tenderheart Bear™ (red heart), Cheer Bear ™ (rainbow on tummy), and Secret Bear ™ (heart shaped padlock on tummy).

15" (standing) peach plush Secret Bear ™ with topknot curl has white snout, paw pads, and heart shaped foot soles. Plastic eyes, pink plastic heart-shaped nose, floss mouth. Round white tummy has a stitched on red heart shaped padlock. Red plastic heart shaped "Care Bears" button on seat. Has tail. Seat tag: "KENNER ®// Cincinnati, Ohio 45202// Secret Bear ™// Care Bears ™// Collection // American Greetings Corp// AGC 1985// Made in Taiwan ROC// Patent Pending." This was not one of the original Care Bears series. Book -*Month by Month, A Care Bear Book of Poems*, by Bobbi Katz, Illustrated by Bobbi Barto, A Care Bear ™ Book from Random House, © 1984. Bear: $15-$25; book: $1-$5

A trio of Care Bears - From left to right: 13" Good Luck ™ Bear (cut 'n' stuff type); 11" seated peach plush Friend Bear ™ with chubby tummy, and a plastic heart-shaped Care Bear button on her backside, and a 13" bright pink Cheer Bear ™ cut 'n' stuff pillow bear. No company or date tags on any of them. $5-$10 each.

13-1/2" standing pastel blue plush Baby Wish (?) Bear wears a cotton (sewn on) diaper with a tiny pattern of a star inside a blue diaper. Blue plastic heart shaped nose, red plastic Care Bears heart shaped tush button, white plush heart shaped footpads. Unfortunately tag is missing, so exact name and copyright date are unknown to author. This also was not one of the original Care Bears series. Bear: $15-$25

Three small Care Bears™: Cheer Bear™ on the left and Friend Bear™ on the right are decal designs over 1" wood. They can stand by themselves. Wish Bear ™ in the center is a rubbery squeak toy. $2-$5 each.

9" yellow plush-covered Care Bears™ bank. The smiling yellow felt sun on the bear's tummy lifts aside (to the left) to reveal the coin slot. A Velcro® fasteners keeps it closed when not in use. Orange plastic nose, orange felt tongue, and orange footpads of 3 toes and heart shape. Hair is a tuft rather than long silky curl. Inside of body is white plastic round container for money. Tag "Care Bears ™//© 1984 American Greetings Corp.// Cleveland, Ohio// Made in Taiwan. $15-$25.

4-1/2" plastic mug depicts Bedtime Bear™ asleep on a cloud, and Funshine Bear™ swinging from a rainbow, and Tenderheart Bear™ smiling from atop a cloud. Above the rainbow it says "Care Bears ™ Say Have A Bear-rific Day!" "™ and Care Bear characters designs are © 1985 American Greetings Corp., © 1985 Pizza Hut Inc." The Pizza Hut logo is near the mug handle. $1-$5.

A small sampling of Care Bear™ storybooks dating from 1983-1985. $1-$5 each.

A Care Bears™ "Tenderheart Bear" on a birthday card for "Daddy," © 1984 by American Greetings, original price: $1.25.

Love-A-Lot Bear™ and Wish Bear ™ carry signs reading "Caring" and "Sharing" and march around a Gerber "Care Bears decorator nurser" baby bottle. $5 mint in package.

Chapter 3
Baseball Bears

One of the first on-site sources of advertising souvenirs — pennants, trading cards, head bobber dolls, and stuffed animals — was the baseball park. Prices were in the $1 to $2.98 range. Now nearly every baseball team has a uniformed bear for sale at the field. Prices run about $7.50-$12 on-site, and higher (plus tax and shipping) through gift catalogs, such as Carol Wright Gifts®. Baseball bears may also be found hibernating regularly at thrift shops, flea markets, and garage sales. Changes in hometowns and uniforms can help you date your baseball bears.

With the advent of "politically correct," sports teams with names such as Braves, Chiefs, Redskins, Blackhawks, and the Cleveland Indians (chosen in 1915 to honor a Native American ballplayer) whose decades-long team mascot is Chief Wahoo, are under pressure to change their names, mascots, and logos to conform to more accepted nomenclature. Fans seem not as adamant as the protesters since in 1997 the Indians ranked first out of 30 teams in souvenir sales. For collectors, name changes mean that souvenir bruins with politically "incorrect" names will be phased out, and should rise in price in the future.

In addition to souvenir bears, there are the limited edition collector bears made by Cooperstown Bears, which cover vintage teams, special players, and the Negro League. Pick your team or player; they probably have it. Cooperstown Bears recently expanded their bear coverage to resin figurines and the Beansville Bears line of bean bag bears of the various teams.

With beanbag bears all the rage, several companies have come out with beanbag baseball bears. Be on the lookout for LA Dodgers Promo Bears, Salvino's Baseball Bammers, Baseball Big Bammers, and 5" Baby Bammers, Salvino's Yankees set, as well as the Coca Cola baseball polar bear, and Flash's 9" "Express to Cooperstown" bears. Famous player bears have also joined the beanbag ranks.

Take me out to the ball game. Gotta get a bear!

Oakland A's. 6" seated gold plush koala, white ear tuffs, back paw pads, and snout; plastic eyes and nose, red felt tongue. Wearing green cap with yellow brim and pompom, with white "A's" stenciled on. Ribbon leg tag: "Official licensee Major League Baseball, Twins Enterprises Inc." and man at bat logo. Tag reverse: "Handcrafted in China, Twins, Boston, MA, 800-448-5046." $5-$8

Oakland Athletics. 14" seated cinnamon brown plush bear. Shirt and hat are part of body. "A's" on green cap and green and yellow "Athletics" decal on white shirt. Amber plastic eyes, brown velour nose, floss mouth. Tag: "Official Licensee, Major League Baseball" with man at bat logo, "Made in Thailand." Tag reverse: "Steven Smith Stuffed Animals Inc., Brooklyn, NY" with Panda bear logo. $15-$20.

California Angels. 10" standing golden plush bear with white snout, ear linings, and back paw pads; plastic eyes, floss nose and mouth. White uniform with navy blue trim is part of the body. Shirt says "Angels" in red with a gold halo on the "A." Navy blue cap is part of head with sewn on red brim and the halo "A" logo. Side tag: "Steven Smith Stuffed Animals, Inc., Brooklyn, NY 11236, © All rights reserved." Tag reverse: Man at bat logo, "Made in China." $5-$10.

Houston Astros. 7" seated black and white plush panda wearing "Go Astros" button on his chest. Navy blue billed cap (part of his head) has an orange star and white "H" machine embroidered on it. Plastic eyes and nose, red felt tongue. Leg tag: "Steven Smith Stuffed Animals, Inc., Brooklyn." Tag reverse: "Made in Korea." The 14" standing golden plush bear wears removable white pants and V-necked shirt trimmed in blue, with "Astros" in blue on the shirt front. White snout, ear linings, and back paw pads; plastic eyes, small brown velour nose, floss mouth. Hat is the same as the panda. "Steven Smith, Made in Korea" ribbon tag. The 5-1/2" plastic hat is a ballpark souvenir. 7": $5-$10; 14": $10-$15; plastic hat: $1-$3.

Atlanta Braves. 9" soft sculptured cloth body, polyester white uniform trimmed in red, navy blue cap with white "A" logo. "Braves" in red and blue, and red tomahawk on the shirt front. Side tag: "Play by Play, San Antonio, TX, Steven Smith/Sports Enterprise, Brooklyn, NY" Purchased at the ballpark in 1997. Note change of uniform colors. *Courtesy of Jean Laughery, photo by Vivian L. Gery.*

Milwaukee Brewers. 9" bear whose clothes are part of his body. Only his head and left paw are plush. White pants, navy blue shirt, shoes, and cap. Shirt cuffs and belt are red, "Brewers" in white on shirt, and "MB" intertwined in gold on hat. Right hand is glove lifted high for a catch. Hanging loop on head, plastic eyes and nose. Side tag: "Genuine Merchandise by Good Stuff Corp." Tag reverse: "© 1993 Good Stuff Corp, © 1993 MLB." The dated tag increases the price. $12-$20.

Atlanta Braves. On the left 9-1/2" golden plush bear whose clothes are part of his body. White snout, ear linings, and back paw pads, plastic eyes and nose, floss mouth. Navy blue shirt with "Braves" and a tomahawk in red, red cuffs, belt and trim on white pants. Red brimmed navy blue hat has "A" stenciled on in white. Paper tag: "Accept No Substitutes, Genuine Merchandise" and man at bat logo. Tag reverse and side tag: "Genuine Merchandise, Play by Play, Steven Smith/Sports Enterprises, Brooklyn; Made in China." In the center, 9" firmly stuffed bear. Only his head and left hand are plush, the uniform, blue shoes, and hat are part of his body. Left hand is sewn-on glove raised for a catch. Eyes are flat plastic ovals. No tags, but probably made by Good Stuff circa 1993. On the right: 10" bear same description as bear on the left, with the same tags. $10-$15 each. Price expected to rise if "Braves" name is outlawed.

St. Louis Cardinals. 15" seated tan plush firmly stuffed bear, white snout, ear linings, and back paw pads, plastic eyes, brown velour nose, brown floss mouth. Red billed cap has "SL" in white, white shirt with red trim is part of body, has "Cardinals" in red and 2 red birds sitting on a bat. Leg tag: "Steven Smith Stuffed Animals Inc., Brooklyn." Tag reverse: man at bat logo and "Made in China." $15-$25. The 9" sipper bottle is marked "St. Petersburg Cardinals" and on the other side "St. Petersburg Times, Tampa Bay's Largest Newspaper." $4-$6. Of the red plastic hats in front with intertwined "SL," one is a souvenir hat and the other is a bank with closed bottom and slot in the top for coins. $1-$6.

Chicago Cubs. 11" standing tan plush bear, amber plastic eyes, black velour nose, wears blue sleeved white T-shirt with "Cubs ®" in red within a blue circle on its front. Back tag: "Applause ®, Division of Wallace Berrie & Co Inc, Woodland Hills, CA, © 1985 Applause, Made in China." $12-$20. The 7" tall Cubs® cup is from the 1997 Triple A All Star Game, Sec Taylor Stadium, Des Moines, Iowa between Iowa and the Cubs. Cup advertises Coca-Cola as well. $3-$9. The 10" seated white plush bear wears a removable white T-shirt with "Cubs" logo on right front and stuffed blue flannel hat with red pompom and red "C." Plastic eyes, black velour nose. Tush tag front has man at bat logo, and reverse: "Handcrafted in China, Twins, Boston, MA." $10-$15.

Chicago Cubs. 8" standing golden koala with white ear tufts and snout, plastic eyes and nose, and red felt tongue. Canvas shoes are part of his body. Brown leatherette catcher' s glove snaps onto hand. Blue plastic mask is pushed above his forehead, blue hat with red "C" is on the back of his head. Brown leatherette chest protector has blue "Cubs" inside a blue circle. Paper ear tag: "Twins, Boston, MA, Official Licensee (man at bat log) Major League Baseball ®" Tush tag: Logo on front, and on reverse: "Twins, Boston, MA, Made in China." $15-$25.

Chicago Cubs. 9" Beansville Buddies printed cloth beanbag bear in Cubs uniform. Blue bear head on his right sleeve and "Teddy 1" on his uniform back. Blue fabric sewn-on cap has red "C." Paper tag front: "Beansville Buddies," and on the reverse "Chicago Cubs." Leg tag: "Beansville Buddies" Tag reverse: "Made in China, Cooperstown Bears Ltd." $10-$15. Cooperstown Bears has for years been making limited edition plush bears of baseball and other teams and characters. They have recently spread out to wooden nesting baseball team figures, resin figurines of players, and the Beansville line. Beansville bear: $10-$25.

Chicago Cubs. Beanie Baby "Cubbie" brown bear by Ty was given free to Cubs game ticket purchasers. To the surprise of ticket sellers and management, Beanie Baby collectors stood in line for hours to purchase the ticket and get the bear and then did not attend the game. Ty retired Cubbie December 31, 1997. Cubbie with Cubs game promotion card: $75-$100; without the card: $35. Cubbie with a First Generation tag: $350-$500. *Courtesy of Nancy Vanselow.*

Above: **Los Angeles Dodgers.** Far left: 7" golden plush koala with white ear tufts, white snout and back paw pads, plastic eyes and nose, floss mouth and eyebrows, red felt tongue. Blue chest button says "Go Dodgers" in white. Blue billed cap, sewed to his head, has "LA" stenciled in white on the front. Leg tag back: "© 1985 Koala-T Products Inc." Tag front: "Handcrafted by Koala-T Products Inc, Hollywood, CA, Made in Korea." $8-$15. Second from left: 8" seated golden koala with very furry white ear tufts, wears removable white shirt trimmed in blue with "Dodgers ®" in blue script. Shirt has Velcro® closure in the back. Hat and body tag same as 7" koala. Paper tag: "Official Dodgers Koala Bear" with picture of koala in front of a red heart. Tag back: "© 1985 Koala-T Products Inc, an official licensee of the Los Angeles Dodgers." $10-$20. Second from right: 7" seated tan plush koala with plastic eyes and nose. Arms are flat flaps. Wears blue "Go Dodgers" chest button, and blue billed cap (part of his head) with "LA" in white flocking. Tush tag: "Handcrafted by © California Stuffed Toys, Los Angeles, CA 90023, Made in Taiwan." Far right: 10" standing light brown plush koala bear with head turned to the right, white snout and ear tufts, red felt tongue, black plastic eyes and nose, floss smile. Plush is short pile and feels like velour. White shirt is part of body, has light blue ribbon cuff trim, and "Dodgers" in blue script. Unreadable body tag. $8-$20.

Right: **Los Angeles Dodgers.** 13" seated brown short pile plush bear, with white snout, ear linings, and back paw pads, plastic eyes, brown velour nose, and brown floss mouth. His white shirt, trimmed in blue, is part of his body. It says "Dodgers" in blue script across his chest. Blue billed baseball cap with "LA" stenciled on. Tush tag: "Steven Smith Stuffed Animals Inc., Brooklyn" Tag reverse: man at bat logo and "Made in Thailand." $10-$15.

San Francisco Giants. Two sizes dressed alike with same body tags: 10" standing golden plush, whose clothes are part of his body. Shirt has "Giants" decal on the front. Blue baseball cap has intertwined "SF" in orange. Very softly stuffed. Paper tag front: "Official Licensee, Major League Baseball ®" and man at bat logo. Reverse: "Steven Smith Stuffed Animals Inc. (with address), Made in China." Identical 14" standing bear, Body tag: "Steven Smith," man at bat logo, "Made in China." Far right: 7" seated white plush bear with plastic eyes, floss nose, black neck ribbon, and black cap with orange pompom and intertwined orange "SF." Ribbon tush tag: Man at bat logo, "Official Licensee of Major League Baseball ®, Twins Enterprises, Inc." Tag reverse: "Handcrafted in China." $10-$15 for 10" & 14", $5-$8 for 7".

Cleveland Indians. 13" standing golden plush bear in red trimmed white uniform that is part of his body. Shirt says "Indians" in red, blue hat with red bill has a decal of Chief Wahoo on it. Paper and tush tags say the same: "Genuine Merchandise, Beware of Substitutes, Manufactured by Steven Smith/Sports Enterprises, Brooklyn, NY, Made in China." Ordered in 1998 from Carol Wright Gifts catalog, price: $6.95 plus shipping/handling/tax. If the "Indians" name and "Chief Wahoo" are abolished the prices are expected to rise. $12-$18.

New York Mets. 13" golden plush bear with white snout, ear linings and footpads. White and blue striped uniform with blue trim is part of his body. A blue and red "Mets" decal is stuck to his uniform chest. Blue cotton hat, part of his head, has stitched bill, and red "NY" decal. Plastic eyes and nose and floss mouth. Side tag: "Play-by-Play, Novelty and Toy Company, San Antonio, Texas, Steven Smith/Sports Enterprises, Brooklyn, New York." Tag reverse: "Genuine Merchandise, Accept No Substitutes" and man at bat logo. "Made in China." $15-$18 *Courtesy of Peggy Monahan*.

New York Mets. 20" seated honey brown short pile plush bear, 1" plastic eyes, brown velour nose, brown floss smile, white muzzle, ear linings, and back paw pads. White and thin blue striped cotton shirt is part of his body. Shirt says "Mets" in blue outlined with orange. Blue baseball cap with orange felt "NY" letters. Leg tag: "Steven Smith Stuffed Animals Inc." man at bat logo, and "Made in Thailand." The 11" standing brown plush bear (left front) has white snout, ear linings, and back paw pads, plastic eyes, light brown velour nose, brown floss mouth. He wears a removable cotton, V-necked, blue and white striped shirt with "Mets" machine embroidered on the front. His blue cap, with felt bill, is machine embroidered with an orange "NY." Tush tag: "Steven Smith Stuffed Animals" and "Made in Korea." The 14" butterscotch plush bear (right front) wears removable cotton blue and white striped V-necked shirt with "Mets" printed on the front. Cap is part of his head; cap bill is faded felt. Tush tag same as 11". Their eyes really seem to see. 20": $20; 11": $12-$15; 14": $15-$18.

New York Mets. Up to Bat 4" baseball bear in blue plastic helmet, blue and white striped glued-on pants and shirt, holding bat, tan plush bear head, black plastic shoes. Paper tag: "Official Licensee Major League Baseball ®" with man at bat logo. Tag reverse: "The MLB Super Clip-Ons, Squeeze my shoulders, turn my head, clip me everywhere, © Major League Baseball 1980, Made in Korea Exclusively for Charles Zadeh's Creative Toys International Inc., Fifth Ave, New York." $10-$15.

San Diego Padres. 10" golden plush bear. White uniform, trimmed in navy blue, is part of his body. "Padres" in blue on his shirt. Blue hat has white "S" and orange "D" intertwined. Paper tag: front man at bat logo, back "Steven Smith Stuffed Animals, Made in China." Side tag same information. $8-$15.

Baltimore Orioles. 9" tan plush bear with only the head and left hand of fur. The orange shirt, white pants, and orange shoes are part of the body. Black shirt cuff and belt trim, "Orioles" in black on shirt, orange oriole bird on black cotton billed cap which is stitched to head. Plastic nose and eyes. Tush tag: "Genuine Merchandise, Good Stuff Corp." Tag reverse: "© 1993 Good Stuff Corp, © 1993 MLB." Even though he's dated, missing one eye lowers his value some. $8-$14.

Texas Rangers. 11" gold plush bear with white muzzle, ear linings and foot soles. His uniform forms part of the body. Navy blue shirt has red "Rangers" decal on the front, white pants, red trim at wrists, ankles, and belt. Red cotton billed cap has white "T" decal on the front. Plastic eyes and nose, floss mouth. Side tag: "Play-By-Play//Steven Smith-Sports Enterprises//Made in China." Tag pictures "man at bat" logo. The Rangers play in the Grapefruit League and do their spring training in Port Charlotte, Florida. The bear was available at the stadium or a souvenir kiosk at the Port Charlotte Town Center Mall (for a limited time) priced at $7.50. Current value $8-12. *Courtesy of Peggy Monahan.*

Cincinnati Reds. In the center 14" standing gold plush bear whose clothes form his body. White uniform with red sleeves, belt, and leg trim. "Reds" on the shirt, and white "C" on the red baseball cap. No tags but resembles "Indians" bear by Steven Smith Stuffed Animals. $10-$14. (From 1996 to 1998 catalogs from Carol Wright Gifts offered uniformed bears with team logos from all the teams.) Right and left are twin 7" seated white plush bears with suction cups on their paws and a hanging loop on their hats. Plastic eyes and nose, wears stuffed red cap with white "C" and white shirt with red trim and "Cincinnati Reds ®" and depicts a runner with a baseball for his head. Shirt has Velcro® closing in back. Tush tag: front has man at bat logo, back: "Twins Ent. Inc., Boston, MA, Product of China." $15-$18 each.

Texas Rangers. 2-1/2" white molded, flocked bear wearing navy blue hat with red "T" and holding a navy pennant with "Rangers" on it in red. Inset eyes, beige paw pads. Two stickers on the bottom. First sticker is man at bat logo "Officially Licensed, Major League Baseball ®." Second sticker: "Russ ®, Made in Hong Kong." $5-$10.

Cincinnati Reds. 13" standing plush black and white Panda. Red shirt and white/red striped pants and matching cap are part of the bear's body. Black cotton sewn on belt. Red "C" on cap. Part of shirt decal is missing, lowering the value somewhat. Amber plastic eyes and black plastic nose. Side tag says: "Genuine Merchandise, Accept No Substitute" with man at bat logo, "Made in China." Tag reverse: "Play-by-Play Toys and Novelties, San Antonio, Texas, Steven Smith/Sports Enterprises, Brooklyn, New York, Made in China." $8-$12.

Boston Red Sox. 7" seated light brown bear with white snout, ear linings, and back paw pads, plastic eyes, brown plastic nose, red felt tongue. Arms are flat flaps of plush. Bear wears red and white "Red Sox" chest button, and navy blue cap with a red "B" machine embroidered on it. Tush tag: "Steven Smith Stuffed Animals, Made in Korea." $8-$12.

Chicago White Sox. 11" brown plush bear (head and right paw), amber plastic eyes, tiny black plastic nose, floss mouth. Brown plastic catcher's mitt on left paw is part of body. White and black striped uniform is part of body as are white socks and black shoes with soft rubber cleats on soles. "Sox" in white on black cap and in black on uniform left breast. Tag: "Genuine Merchandise, Accept No Substitutes" with man at bat logo and "Made in China." Tag reverse: "Play-by-Play" and "Steven Smith/ Sports Enterprises." No copyright date. $10-$17. *Courtesy of Peggy Monahan.*

Colorado Rockies. 11" tan plush bear, with oval plastic eyes, brown plastic nose, cream snout. His navy top and shoes, and white pants form part of his body. Only his head and left hand are plush. Raised right gloved hand has caught a ball. "Rockies" is on his shirt, and a silver "R" is on his navy blue hat. Paper tag front: "Sports Stuff ™, Genuine Merchandise, Accept No Substitutes." Reverse: "Official Licensed Product, Sports Stuff, A Division of Good Stuff Corporation, Long Island, NY, © 1992 Good Stuff Corp., Made in China." The body tag says "© 1993, Good Stuff." $10-$15.

Mark McGwire. 13" plush bear called "One Fur the Record Books" represents homerun king Mark McGwire. Patch on his back says: "Home Run #62, St. Louis 9-8-98." Individually numbered, he came with replica autographed baseball and stand. By Gallery Teddy Bears, issue price: $55 (included shipping).

New York Yankees. 7" seated panda wears "Go Yankees" chest button and a navy blue cap with "NY" machine embroidered in white. Black plastic eyes and nose, red felt tongue. Tush tag is unreadable but he resembles the Astros panda who was made by Steven Smith Stuffed Animals. $5-$10. The 12" standing light brown bear with tan snout and back paw pads, wears a navy blue sleeved white T-shirt with "Yankees ®" and a bat in red. Navy baseball cap has ear holes and excellently stitched 1-3/4" white "NY" on it. Plastic eyes and nose. Tush tag: "Trudy ™, Norwalk, CT, USA, Made in Korea, © 1983 Trudy Toys." This same basic bear was used for State Farm Insurance shirts. $12-$16.

Chapter 4

Other Beary Good Sports

Baseball is not the only sport to utilize bears as souvenirs or for promotion. Football, hockey, basketball, auto racing, and even the World Wrestling Federation and the Olympics have issued highly collectible bears in uniform. And let's not forget the collegiate teams.

Beanbag bears have invaded the entire sports world. If beanbag bears are your passion, you have dozens (and before long, hundreds) to choose from. Salvino's Classic Collectibles Signature Series features authorized bears signed by Joe Montana and Joe Namath, soon to be followed by other famous players. Salvino's also offers a set of six bears called Super Bowl Bammers. Other NFL bears include NFL Bammers, Premium Pro Bears ™ and Limited Treasurers Pro Bears ™ which will be retired at the end of each playing season. Basketball is represented by the Los Angeles Lakers Legends beanbag bear series and Coast to Coast's Nickname Series I "Heroez® Collection" featuring. White Chocolate, The Mailman, The Answer, Diesel, The Admiral, The Glove, and a limited edition Michael Jordan bear. Coca Cola's Heritage Collection polar bear gets sporty in football, golf, and skiing outfits. Hockey fans will be pleased to hear about Salvino's hockey set. World Championship Wrestling's beanbag buddies include Hollywood Hogan and Konnan; the World Wrestling Federation contenders are called "Bears With Attitude."

Pro Bear. In 1995, 21" freestanding bears weighing in at 3 pounds, were made of high quality plush and called Pro-Bears, seen in this advertisement. Fully clad in the official uniforms, equipment, and authentic logo detail of every professional sports team in the NBA, NFL, NHL, and Major League Baseball, they were available from fine department, gift, and specialty stores. By 1998 the 800 phone number for Pro-Bear had been discontinued. (A few on display at Teddy Bear Museum of Naples, Florida.)

Football

Buffalo Bills. 11" light brown plush bear (head and front paws), plastic eyes and nose, floss mouth. Uniform of blue shirt, white pants with red trim, and blue shoes are part of body. "BILLS" is stenciled in red and white across the shirt front. Tag: "Team NFL" and "Good Stuff." Tag reverse: "© 1993 Good Stuff Corp." $10-$15.

Chicago Bears. Team NFL bear ornament: 3" rust colored polyresin bear wears blue hat and shirt with orange trim and orange "Bears" on it Packaged in cellophane-front box which says "NFL Officially licensed product, Russ®, Bears from the Past™, Russ, Berrie and Company, Inc., Oakland, New Jersey, Made in China, ™ © 1994 NFLP." They were listed in 1996 Carol Wright Gifts catalog for $9.95 plus shipping/ handling/tax. All teams were available. Current: $12-$16.

Chicago Bears. This 16" white plush bruiser bruin joined the Chicago Bears in 1986. His hat with ear holes, and blue sweater with gold "C" are removable, if you dare. *Courtesy of Ginny Kreitler.*

Kansas City Chiefs. This little bear literally lost his head over the game. Shoulders to bottom measure 3". Stuffed round bottom, round-top wooden clothespins for arms, covered with red and white "Chiefs" helmet print fabric. No tags. Possibly homemade, maybe as favors for football luncheon. $1-$4 as is.

Colts/Rams. 4" "NFL Super Clip-Ons" bears. On the left in blue flocked shirt and white pants is the Baltimore Colts bear, and on the right in navy shirt and yellow pants the Los Angeles Rams bear. © 1981. Paper tags same as Cardinals clip-on bear. $5-$10.

St. Louis Cardinals. 4" "NFL Super Clip-Ons" bear with maroon flocked shirt and gray pants, plastic "people" hands and shoes, light tan plush head, white plastic helmet with red cardinal head. Paper tag reverse says: "Squeeze my shoulders, turn my head, clip me everywhere, © 1981 The NFL Properties, Inc., US Pat. No., Made in Korea exclusively for Charles Zadeh's Creative Toys International Inc, New York, NY." $5-$10.

Colts/Seahawks. Pair of 2-1/2" molded, flocked bears, with inset eyes, by Russ®. Both are missing their team pennants. White bear with pink back paw pads wears blue hat with "Colts" in white. Tan bear with peach back paw pads wears blue hat with "Seahawks" in green. Two stickers on each bottom. First sticker: "NFL Officially Licensed Product." Second sticker: "Russ®, Made in Hong Kong." $4-$9 each.

Philadelphia Eagles. 4" "NFL Super Clip-Ons" bear in Philadelphia Eagles uniform, green flocked shirt, gray pants, white plastic shoes, and green plastic helmet with white eagle wings. Tan plush bear head. © 1981. Paper tags the same as Cardinals clip-on bear. $5-$10

Miami Dolphins. 8" brown bear has plush head and hands. His green and orange cotton uniform and shoes form the rest of his body. Eyes and nose are plastic. A hanging loop is sewn to his head. Plasticized side tags have the "NFL Officially Licensed Product™" Seal and "Good Stuff ®" logo. Tag reverse reads "Made in China © 1997 Good Stuff Corp." This bear has a different look from the other sports bears. $6-$12.

Back view of Miami Dolphins 8-inch bear, ©1997

Atlanta Falcons. 10" (standing) pink plush bear (probably blushing) with plastic eyes and nose. His removable white T-shirt has black falcon wings on each shoulder, and number 95 on his shirt back. He has two ears, one is cocked back to hear the cheering. His only tag says "Made in China." $5-$8.

New York Giants. A bruiser of a bruin, 10" brown plush bear with 7" shoulder-span holds felt football. His blue shirt with red sleeve stripes and "Giants" patch, white pants and shoes are part of his body. Oval eyes, black velour nose, tan snout and ear linings. Side tag: "Good Stuff" Reverse: "© 1991 Good Stuff Corporation, Long Island City, NY, Made in China." Paper tag missing. $10-$15.

New York Jets. 9" standing brown plush bear, with suction cups on his front paws, wears a removable shirt with green sleeves and a chest patch that says "Jets" in green above a green Jets helmet. Paper tag front shows a bear juggling football, basketball, and bat over the name "Sports Stuff ™" and "Team NFL." Tush tag: "© 1991 Good Stuff Corp., Long Island City, NY, Made in China." Unfortunately, his paper tag was written on in permanent ink. $8-$15.

New York Jets. On the left, 3-1/2" "NFL Super Clip-Ons" bear in New York Jets uniform, green flocked shirt, white pants, white shoes, green plastic Jets helmet, plastic "people" hands, tan plush bear head. Paper tag: "Squeeze my shoulders, turn my head, clip me everywhere; © 1981 The NFL Properties Inc., Made in Korea exclusively for Charles Zadeh's Creative Toys International Inc, New York, NY." On the right, 2-1/2" molded, white flocked bear with inset eyes and pink back paw pads. He holds green Jets pennant and wears green Jets hat. Marked on bottom with two paper stickers. First sticker says "NFL, Officially Licensed Product." Second sticker reads: "Russ ®, Made in Hong Kong." $4-$10 each.

Front view of Houston Oilers and Seattle Seahawks 4" "NFL Super Clip-Ons" bears showing their faces.

Houston Oilers/Seattle Seahawks. 4" "NFL Super Clip-Ons" bears. On the left in light blue shirt and white pants is the Houston Oilers bear. He is the only one with a body tag: "#104 Oilers." On the right in navy shirt and gray pants is the Seattle Seahawks bruin. © 1981. Paper tags same as Cardinals clip-on bear. $5-$10.

Green Bay Packers/San Diego Chargers. 4" "NFL Super Clip-Ons" bears. On right a Green Bay Packers bear in flocked green shirt, gold pants, and gold plastic helmet. On the right wearing blue flocked shirt, white pants, and blue plastic helmet is the San Diego Chargers bruin. © 1981. Paper tags the same as Cardinals clip-on bear. $5-$10.

Seattle Seahawks. 8" brown plush bear has oval plastic eyes, black plastic nose, and growling teeth on the right side of his beige snout. He carries a felt football. The blue shirt with "Seahawks" in green, white pants, and green/white shoes are part of his body. Paper tag: juggling bear logo and "Sports Stuff ™" and "Team NFL." Leg tag: "Good Stuff" on front, and on reverse: "© 1992 Good Stuff Corp., Made in China." $10-$15.

Washington Redskins™. 23" pot bellied bear made from Redskins print fabric with an Indian head in a circle and Redskins written in red. No tags. Well made but probably a homemade product. A good size for hugging. The 4" glass to his left says "1937-1987, 50, Washington Redskins" on the front. Glass reverse: "NFL" on shield with football. Bear: $15 up; glass: $4-$12. Prices are expected to rise if team name is abolished.

Minnesota Vikings™. 12" tan plush bear with black grease paint at the bottom of his oval plastic eyes, has 8" shoulder-span. Purple shoes, white pants, gold belt, and purple shirt with "Vikings ™" stenciled on in gold, are part of his body. Side tag: "Team NFL, Good Stuff." Tag reverse: "© 1993 Good Stuff Corp., Made in China." Paper tag missing. $12-$18.

Super Bowl XX. 11" standing, light brown bear, pale yellow snout and back paw pads, plastic eyes and nose. Shirt is a nylon pull-on with navy sleeves, white front and back with "Super Bowl XX" over a red bear head, and "Champions 1986" on the front. Leg tag: "Trudy, Norwalk, CT, USA, Made in Korea, © 1983 Trudy Toys." Paper tag: "NFL Officially Licensed Product, Trudy Official Licensee." Reverse: "© 1980." Original price: $2. Same basic bear as State Farm Insurance: $15-$20. *Courtesy of Shirley Taylor.*

Basketball

Philadelphia 76ers™. 9" gold plush bear with googly-look eyes, brown plastic nose, floss smile. His red shirt, white pants with blue trim, suntanned flannel legs, white socks, and red shoes are part of his body. His shirt front has a basketball with "76ers" on it. Side tag: "Good Stuff" and NBA logo. Tag reverse: "Made in China, © 1993 Good Stuff Corp." $4-$10.

Dallas Mavericks. 10" standing cheerleader bear. Only her head and front paws are plush, legs are flesh colored cotton, navy blue and green outfit, green underpants, and shoes are part of her body. She holds blue and green yarn pom-poms, wears a green bow near her ear, has flirty black felt eyelashes, plastic eyes and nose, and floss mouth and eyebrows. The logo on her shirt says "Dallas Mavericks™" with a green basketball and a white cowboy hat hanging from the top right point of an "M." Waist tag: "Play-By-Play, Made in China." $10-12. *Courtesy of Peggy Monahan.*

Detroit Pistons. 9" standing golden bear with felt eyelashes and floss eyebrows, plastic eyes and nose, floss mouth, red ribbon stitched to her ear. She wears a red and blue cheerleader outfit, red/white/blue shoes, and shakes red and blue pompoms to cheer on her team. Red panties under her skirt and suntanned people legs. Waist tag: "Play-By-Play ® Toys & Novelties, San Antonio, Texas, Made in China." Paper tag front: "Official NBA Licensed Product®" with red/white/blue basketball logo. Tag reverse: holograph of "Official Licensee" and number. "Distributed by Play-By-Play® Toys & Novelties, © 1994 NBA Properties Inc., Made in China." $12-$18.

Hockey

NHL Blue Line Bears™. 21" beige plush bears dressed in National Hockey League uniforms. Far left Chicago Blackhawks, second from left Toronto Maple Leafs, second from right Boston Bruins, far right Detroit Red Wings. These bears were made by Cooperstown Bears in a limited edition of 2,000 each. They appear in the Cooperstown Bears 1998 catalog.

Hershey's Bears. 10" seated brown plush bear, with tail, wears a white shirt with a hockey playing bear and "Hershey's Bears ®" in brown. Darker plush snout, ear linings, and back paw pads, plastic eyes and nose. Leg tag: bear logo "ASI 32960" Tag reverse: "Made in China." Paper tag: "Officially Licensed Product, American Hockey League, AHL." Was purchased at Hershey Park stadium 1998 for $12.50 plus tax. Stuffed bears have been available since 1991. The Hershey Arena was built in 1937 and is the oldest hockey arena still functioning. The team is a separate franchise from Hershey Foods.

Chicago Blackhawks. Back view of 7" bear showing the round black pillow that pops out an opening in the back of the bear. A profile of the mascot Indian with colorful feathers in his hair is centered on the pillow.

Chicago Blackhawks. 7" golden brown plush bear with amber plastic eyes and black velour nose, floss mouth. His bow tie, paw pads and ear linings all have the Blackhawks Indian head print. Tag: "Official Licensed Product, NHL" Tag reverse: "Pillow Pal ™, Reversible Teddy Bear, Officially licensed Product of the NHL, Made in China." $10-$15. Prices may rise if team name is abolished.

Auto Racing

Indy 500. 10" standing beige plush bear with upraised arms wears blue sleeved shirt (part of his body) with "INDY 500" stitched in large red letters. White snout and ear linings, plastic eyes and nose, red felt tongue protruding. Leg tag: "Sport Services Inc, Canoga Park, Calif., Raceway Services, Indianapolis, IN., Made in Taiwan." Paper ear tag: "Officially Licensed Product, Indianapolis Motor Speedway ®." $10-$18. NASCAR observed its 50th anniversary in 1998. *Courtesy of Robert Reed, Antique & Collectible News Service.*

Daytona 88. 12" standing light brown bear with oval plastic eyes, dark brown plastic nose, and open mouth lined with felt. Wears jeans with straps, and a red neckerchief with white dots. On the front waist of his jeans is a white patch with "Daytona '88'" embroidered in red. No body or paper tags. He appears to be the same bear and jeans used for Shoney's. $8-$15.

Other Sports

Fishing. 16" L.H. Bear from the Orvis catalog ("A sporting tradition since 1856.") L.H. Bear was introduced in 1991— named for the then Orvis Company CEO Leigh H. Perkins — and retired in 1997. Approximately 1,000 L.H. Bears were sold through the catalog during that period. The bear was inspired by the 1975 illustrated book, "The Bear With The Orvis Rod," written and illustrated by A.D. Read. Of soft acrylic fur, L.H. came attired in red fishing hat, vest, miniature Orvis graphite rod, two hand-tied trout flies, and the storybook (price: $65). Bare Bear, without accessories ($29), just the book ($12). An 18" Ojibwa-made birch bark canoe ($32.50) and miniature 4-1/2" x 3" wicker creel ($9.95) were also available for L.H. Bear. All made in the U.S.A. *Photo and information courtesy of Robert Dagley, Orvis®.*

Wrestling. 15" standing gold plush bear with white front paw pads, plastic eyes and nose, wears yellow plastic shoes with red laces, a yellow body suit with "Hulk Rules" in red, and a black leatherette belt with "WWF" (World Wrestling Federation) in gold. Leg tag: "© 1989 Titan Sports Inc, Hulk Hogan ™, Hulkamania ™, and Hulkster™ are trademarks of the Marvel comics Group, licensed exclusively to Titan Sports Inc., WWF ®, Made in Taiwan." $10-$20.

Olympics

Summer Olympics, 1980. Copy of advertisement for 7" Misha ™ bear, the mascot of the 1980 Olympics in Moscow. In November 1980, The Doll Factory in West Palm Beach, Florida offered a limited supply for $6.95 plus $2 shipping. Misha was also made in 11", 16", and 21" sizes. The U.S. boycotted the Moscow Olympics in protest of Russia's invasion of Afghanistan and R. Dakin reacted by stopping production and distribution of Misha. *Courtesy of Kerra Davis.*

1980 Misha. 8" non-jointed brown plush bear with beige tummy, snout, and ear linings. Plastic eyes have wide-eyed look, black plastic nose and floss smile. He wears a light blue Olympic swim team pin (shows Misha swimming) on his ear, and a belt with multi-color ribbon back and five metal intertwined Olympic rings in front. Misha ™ (all sizes) has black felt toes and a small tail. Tush tag: "Misha ™, © Organizing Committee of the 1980 Olympic Games in Moscow, Image Factory Sports Inc, R. Dakin & Co." Tag reverse: "R. Dakin & Co, San Francisco, CA, Product of Korea." Paper folder ear tag has picture of Misha on the front, and inside: "Misha ™ is the Official Mascot of the 1980 Moscow Olympic Games. A portion of the purchase price of Misha ™ goes to the support of your country's Olympic Committee." Tag back: "© 1979 Image Factory Sports Inc., R. Dakin & Co, Product of Korea." A 1994 price guide suggested a $75-$80 value for 11" Misha.
Small Misha courtesy of Nancy Vanselow.

1980 Misha. From left to right 21" Misha with Olympic belt, added Russian pin; 21" Misha missing Olympic belt; 8" Misha with Olympic belt and paper tag; and 16" Misha missing Olympic belt. "©1979, R. Dakin & Co, Product of Korea." *Courtesy of Bonnie and Larry Vaughan.*

Russian postage stamp issued at Christmastime 1980 shows Misha with a lighted Christmas tree and a Santa Claus stamp.

Olympics (Ski Team). 15" white plush bear with plastic eyes and black velour nose, wears a red knitted scarf and red cap with a big white pompom. Both display the "U.S. Ski Team" symbol. Tush tag: "Commonwealth Toy and Novelty Co., New York, NY, © 1986, Made in Korea." In 1987 the Nestle company offered this official U.S. Ski Team mascot bear for two proofs-of-purchase from their chocolate candy bar products, plus $7.95. (Tough job to have to eat that product!! says this chocoholic.) He's missing his paper ear tag, which pictured a bear holding the U.S. Ski Team symbol. $12-$20.

Olympics (Sport Unknown). 9-1/2" brown flannel bear with hair tuff, plastic eyes and nose, floss mouth and toe separations. The cotton one piece outfit he wears is part of his body (shirt only). Back waist tag reads: "A, ACE Inc, 1996 Ace Novelty Company Inc." Tag reverse: "Official Licensed Product 36USC380...Made in China." $10-$15

Olympics (Calgary). "Hidy and Howdy" advertising mascot bears for the Calgary (Canada) 1988 Olympic games. A popular pair, Hidy and Howdy are all original and "bear" their original tags. Large and small size pairs were produced. Actual measurements unknown to author. *Courtesy of Jacqueline Wilson, Photo by Russ Wilson.*

Olympics (Boxing). 10" standing brown flannel bear wears red plastic boxing gloves and shorts which are red and white striped on one side, with "USA" and the Olympic rings on the blue side. He has a little tuft of hair standing up between his ears. Oval plastic eyes, brown plastic nose, stitching defines toes. Paper tag shows Olympic medal with "USA" and Olympic rings, and "U.S. Olympic Team, Official Licensed Product." Waist tag: "© 1995 Ace Novelty Co. Inc." Tag reverse: "© 1995 United States Olympic Committee, Ace Novelty Co Inc, Authorized Licensee, Made in China." An identical bear's body tag says "© 1996." His face is slightly slimmer and his muzzle more pointed. $12-$16 each.

College Teams

University of Miami. 3-1/2" orange plush covered Stork with orange plastic bill and feet, plastic eyes, wears dark green velour vest with "Hurricanes" stenciled in orange on the back. White plastic visored helmet has yellow and green stripe from front to back and an orange and green "U" each side. His paws have springs so they can grip a lapel or car visor. $2-$5.

University of Miami. 9" standing bright orange plush bear, plastic eyes and nose, white removable shirt says "University of Miami" under a striding stork in green shirt with white "M." Leg tag only lists contents and "Made in China." College located in Coral Gables, Florida. $5-$10.

University of Florida. 12" butterscotch plush bear wears removable orange shirt with 2-1/4" white pin with "Florida Gator's" and a green alligator wearing an orange shirt with an "F" on the front. Pin is pinned and glued down. Waist tag: "Sound Around Ltd, Plymouth, MI 48170, Made in China." School is located in Gainesville, Florida. $5-$10.

Florida State University. 8" (seated) white plush bear, plastic eyes and nose, floss mouth, dressed in removable slip-on maroon knitted sweater with "FSU" in gold on the front and "Seminoles" knitted in gold across the back. Tush tag: "Acme ® Premium Supply Corp © 1991" Reverse: "Made in China." $6-$12.

University of Florida. Pair of 11" Florida Gators ® Athletics cheerleaders in red and blue outfits. He holds white plastic megaphone, and she holds red and blue yarn pompoms. She has black felt eyelashes. Body tags: " 1996 Play-By-Play Toys & Novelties, San Antonio, TX, Made in China." Paper tags: "Official Licensed Collegiate Products." $14-$20 each. *Courtesy of L. Victor Desguin.*

University of Indiana. 10" red plush bear has plastic eyes and nose. Removable white T-shirt has the red intertwined "UI" on the front. Tush tag gives no manufacturer, only "All new material, 100% polyester fiber, Made in China." $5-$8

Florida State University. 8-1/2" felt jacket patch with brown plush on the bear. Red and yellow hat says "FSU" and shirt says "Seminoles." $5.

University of Nebraska. 12" golden plush bear with white snout, ear linings, and back paw pads, plastic eyes, black velour nose, and floss mouth. He wears a removable red shirt with a glued-on 2-1/4" white wooden circle which says "Go Big Red." Waist tag: "Sound Around Ltd., Plymouth, MI 48170, Made in China." Paper tag missing. $5-$10.

North Carolina State. 6" seated white plush bear with 3-1/2" white cord loop on his head. Plastic eyes and black plastic nose. Wears white sleeved red shirt that says "N.C. State Wolf Pack" Leg tag: "Sporty Bear." Tag reverse: "© 1988 Sporty Bear, Made in Korea." $5-$10.

Texas. 13" light brown bear in brown boots, blue vest and red hat with blue "A" above the brim, has suction cups on his front paws and boots. He appears cross-eyed, has freckles, and two protruding teeth. Pink ear linings, black plastic nose. Leg tag: "School Days, 800-803-4343, Designed by Niska." Tag reverse: "Made in China." Paper ear tag: "Officially Licensed Collegiate Products." $5-$10.

USC (University of Southern California). 18" seated golden plush bear, large soft leatherette nose, toothy growling smile, cross-eyed, red felt shirt with "USC" and school emblem in gold paint. Unjointed, firmly stuffed. Leg tag: "Shell Made in USA, Finished in China, Ace Novelty, Los Angeles-Chicago-Seattle." Paper tag is missing. $8-$12.

UCLA (University of California at Los Angeles). 8" seated bear of flannel-like fabric with felt ears. Light blue shirt is part of his body and says "UCLA" in yellow paint He's cross-eyed, has brown plastic nose, and felt toothy grin. Paper tag front: "Collegiate Licensed Product," and "© 1984 CC/ICE, A Product of Ace Novelty Co Inc." Tush tag: "Ace Novelty Co Inc, Los Angeles-Chicago-Seattle, Made in China." On the left: 11" seated tan plush bear whose flannel-like shirt is part of his body. Shirt says "UCLA." Cross-eyed, black leatherette nose, shows a mouth full of teeth. Tush tag is same as 8". Missing his paper tag. $5-$10 each. *Small bear courtesy of Lavonne Morrell.*

Harvard/Indiana. 11" seated plush bear from Harvard, and 8" seated flannel-like bear from Indiana. Both are "© 1984. Descriptions," paper and tush tags are the same as the UCLA bears. These two both wear red shirts. Indiana has an extra tush tag, in English and French, that says "made by Ont. Reg. No., Made in China." $5-$10 each.

Chapter 5

Charitable Bears

Bears and kids, of all ages, have a natural affinity. Organizations nationwide have hopped aboard the bear mania bandwagon and instituted programs using a bear as their logo, as a gift for traumatized children, or to get their educational goals noticed by the public.

Police prowl cars, and fire and rescue units regularly carry stuffed bears to give to children involved in accidents. November is called "Teddy Bear Goodwill Month" by owners of a Donut and Deli shop in Canada who offer free donuts to anyone bringing in a new teddy bear to be given to local police and hospitals. As one of their projects chapter members of Telephone Pioneers of America sew cloth "comfort" bears. The nonprofit Bearing Gifts Foundation, headquartered in Monmouth, New Jersey, distributes new and barely used bears at home and abroad. Good Bears of the World, founded in 1973, disseminates bears worldwide to comfort ill and lonely children and adults. In February 1999 Target Stores and Hershey joined together to sponsor "Helping Hugs," a program (begun in 1991) which supplies millions of teddy bears to the American Red Cross and Emergency Medical Technicians to comfort children in crisis situations. A portion of the sales of Hershey's™ Kisses Valentine candies was donated to help underwrite the program. The late Princess Diana's favorite charities benefit from the sale of several bears, with part of the proceeds going to the charitable causes.

American Red Cross. 12" seated white plush bear with plastic eyes, velour nose, floss mouth, wearing a red neck bow and removable red-sleeved white shirt with "American Red Cross" below a red cross. Clara Barton (1821-1912) founded the American Red Cross. The international parent organization, for the care of the sick and wounded in war, was formed in Geneva in 1864, and adopted the red Geneva cross as a badge of neutrality. *Courtesy of Fredye Cochran, RN, from the collection of the late Blanche King.*

United Way. 9" black and white plush panda wears a removable red shirt with the message: "Spread the Good News! The United Way." Plastic eyes, black plastic nose, floss mouth, white tail. Tush tag: "Logo Bear © 1985, New York, NY, Made in Korea." Before being known as the "United Way," this fund raising effort was called the Community Chest. $5-$10.

Good Bears of the World. "Silver" the 25th anniversary bear of Good Bears of the World was issued in 1994 in a limited edition of 5,000. Individually numbered, he came with a special certificate, a hang tag with the history of GBW, and a black neck ribbon with the GBW logo. Issue price was $16. An anniversary cloisonné pin was available for $5. Created in 1969 and chartered in Bern, Switzerland in 1973. GBW celebrates October 27th as Good Bear Day to honor President Teddy Roosevelt. The organization' s aim is "to put the comfort of a teddy bear into the arms and hearts of every traumatized child or lonely, forgotten adult in the world." GBW publishes a newsletter called "Bear Tracks" that keep Dens informed of what other Dens are doing, and offer bear related items for purchase or fund raising. In 1994 the Third Edition of the Official Good Bear (11-1/2" dark brown plush by Muffin Enterprises) was manufactured for use in the program.

Princess Diana. Purple velvet "Beanie Baby" with purple neck ribbon and pink rose machine embroidered on right chest. Paper Ty tag: "Princess ™, Like an angel, she comes from Heaven above, She shared her compassion, her pain, her love, She only stayed with us long enough to teach The world to share, to give, to reach.// Net profits of Ty from this collectible will be donated to the DIANA, PRINCESS OF WALES MEMORIAL FUND.//The Beanie Baby Collection ®, © Ty Inc, Oak Brook, IL, © Ty Europe Ltd, Fareham, Hants P015 5TX U.K.//© Ty Canada, Aurora, Ontario." The Memorial Fund uses Diana's signature as a logo. There were three issues of the Diana bear. Issue #1 is 9" tall, says "PVC pellets" on the tush tag, and is valued at $245. Issue #2 and #3 are 8" tall, say "PE pellets," and are valued at $85. Because it was thought the first issue was a one-time limited edition, prices up to $600 were paid. *Information courtesy of Nancy Vanselow, Bear courtesy of Cerissa Katyryniuk.*

Helping Hugs. A Hershey sponsored project in January-February 1999, which was established in 1991. Part of the purchase price of any Hershey product prior to Valentine's Day raised dollars to buy Teddy Bears for use by the American Red Cross and Emergency Medical Technicians.

Princess Diana. An advertisement for "England's Rose," a white plush teddy wearing a lacy tiara, and a blue velvet bow fastened with a faux sapphire and diamond pin. On her right foot is an embroidered white rose with blue leaves. Plastic eyes and floss nose and mouth. This handcrafted teddy bear, designed by artist Lenore DeMent, was created to celebrate the life of the late Princess Diana. Limit of one to a customer, © 1999 by Gallery Teddy Bears, no size is given. Issue purchase price of $68 included shipping and a donation made in the purchaser's name to one of the Princess of Wales' charities.

Star. 8" seated brown plush bear with beige muzzle, paw pads, and ear linings. Plastic eyes and brown velour nose. Brown neck ribbon with paper tag which reads: "Because We Care." Tush tag has a shooting star, the word "Star" and "San Francisco." Tag reverse: "© 1994 Giant Star Corporation, Made in China." It is not known exactly what charity this represents. $8-$12.

Paralyzed Veterans of America. 8-1/4" "Gift of Love." This 1997, 50th anniversary collector plate commemorates 50 years of Paralyzed Veterans of America helping those who served our country. The story behind the plate: "Early one morning, a mother who lost a loved one in Vietnam left a tender gift of love — a teddy bear — at the Vietnam Veterans Memorial. Throughout the day, other visitors dressed and decorated the bear with their own special gifts — a combat vest, photograph, Purple Heart, flowers." The plate, limited to 45 firing days, was painted by artist Donald Patterson, decorated in the USA, rimmed and individually numbered in hand-applied 24 karat gold. Issue price: $29.95 plus $3.45 shipping. Order limit was one per collector.

Women in Military Service for America Memorial. "Friendly Bear" was created in 1993 to help raise funds for the "Women in Military Service for America Memorial" to be built at the gate of Arlington National Cemetery, Arlington, Virginia. "Friendly" is brown plush and wears a red-sleeved T-shirt with an imprint of the "Women in Our Armed Forces" U.S. postage stamp. Issue price was $15 plus $3 shipping.

Chapter 6

Medical Bears

Hospitals, blood banks, doctor's groups, and pharmaceutical companies employ bears as bearers (pardon the pun) of their messages. Some bears are for comfort, others — like Sir Koff-A-Lot — are therapeutic aids. Many hospital emergency rooms keep donated bears on hand to comfort injured children. A Lions Club in Oregon donated a talking teddy bear to comfort a frightened little boy about to undergo multiple surgery procedures. In 1992 a Florida hospital published its own "Visit To The Hospital" coloring and activities book showing bears as the patient and medical personnel. It explained people, items, or activities a child might expect to encounter as a patient: name bracelet, blood pressure check, X-rays, IVs, meals in bed. That hospital also used a foundation grant to start a "Bearly Sick" child care program for the use of medical personnel and townspeople whose children were too sick to go to school or day care, but not ill enough to be hospitalized. Bearly Sick's program logo was a bear, and a costumed bear visited the children on special occasions. "Jimmy Bear" is the name of the traveling bear from Galveston and Portland Shrine Hospitals. The newest use of bears in the medical field is "Get Better Bear sore throat pops." They look like lollipops, and are less likely than cough drops to be swallowed by children.

Above: **Sir Koff-A-Lot.** This 15" original version of the therapeutic aid bear "Sir Koff-A-Lot" was handcrafted by Carol Bailey of Bailey's Bears, Waynesboro, PA. The bear was the idea of a team of cardiovascular surgeons from Harrisburg, PA, to help their post-operative patients perform required coughing and deep breathing exercises in order to prevent respiratory complications. Sir Koff-A-Lot is solidly stuffed, and his straight back makes a perfect size surgical splint for patients to hold over their incision while they cough. Various colors were available. This one is brown plush with darker ears and paw ads. His white shirt says "Sir Koff-A-Lot" in red above a diagram of what appears to be a heart valve. He wears a red neck bow. *Courtesy of Jean Laughery, photo by Vivian L. Gery.*

Right: **Sir Koff-A-Lot.** The demand for Sir Koff-A-Lot was so great that Ms. Bailey could not keep up with the orders. Muffin Enterprises took over and copyrighted the bear in 1984. This 15" Sir Koff-A-Lot is gray plush with black paw pads and ear linings. His white shirt says on the front: "Sir Koff-A-Lot ™, Regional Heart Institute of Medical Center Hospital, Punta Gorda, Florida." On the shirt back is this poem: "A Cough for your lungs, A Hug for your heart, I'll help you to Bear it, By doing my part.// © Muffin Enterprises 1984." A 1994 magazine photo of "Sir's" shirt had his name and "Speedy Recovery" over a red heart shape. By 1997 "Sir" had been joined by "Kiddie Kub" bear for child patients.

Hospital. This 9" seated brown plush bear wears a red shirt advertising "Women's, Infants' and Children's Center at Plantation General Hospital." The bear has beige ear linings, snout, and back paw pads, plastic eyes, black plastic nose, and floss mouth. Tush tag: "Logo Bear © 1985, New York, NY, Made in Korea." $5-$10.

Hospital. 5-1/2" seated little brown bear wears a removable white shirt stating "Howard Community Hospital, Treating You Well ®" A Velcro® strip closes the shirt back. Leg tag: "Steven Smith Stuffed Animals Inc., Brooklyn, NY, Made in Philippines." Bear was purchased in Indiana. $4-$8.

Hospital. Two plush bears with plastic eyes, small plastic nose, red felt tongue, and neck ribbon. They measure 3" from front to back. On the posterior of each is sewn a label: "Donated by the Plantation Community Hospital." These bears are similar to those made by Telephone Pioneers of America chapter members. $3-$6 each.

Pediatrics. 6" seated all white bear, dressed in removable pink shirt saying "Partners in Pediatrics, Bob Kim MD, George Rada MD." Plastic eyes, tiny black plastic nose, 2" red cord loop on head. Tush tag: bear logo and "ASI 62960" Tag reverse: "Made in Indonesia." (Bear purchased in Indiana.) $3-$6.

Hospital. In 1985 St. Anthony's Medical Center (St. Louis, MO) rewarded new mothers with this cuddly golden brown bear with lavender bow tie. Right foot says "With Love From"; left foot says "St. Anthony's Medical Center." Since having a baby is a drastic step to take to acquire a bear, this one was wangled from the gift shop cashier. *Courtesy of Ginny Kreitler.*

Medical Center. 14"x14" cloth tote bag from "Mercy-Memorial Medical Center Inc, Here for your Health" uses a bear with heart to illustrate their message. The bag was purchased in Indiana. $1-$5.

Blood Bank. 9" seated brown bear wears removable red shirt saying "You're Beary Special, Edison Regional Blood Center." (Florida) Cream snout; ear linings, and back paw pads, plastic eyes and nose, floss mouth. Tush tag: "Logo Bear © 1987, 1992." $5-$10. *Courtesy of Ms. Lee Hoffman.*

Rads.™ This 8" standing golden plush bear is an unbearably cute nurse. Her white uniform is cotton, white shoes and nurse's cap are felt. White cotton legs under the dress are part of her body. Tiny plastic eyes, nearly dime-sized floss nose, peach plush ear linings, red ribbon tie at her Peter Pan collar. Her uniform says "RADS ™" with a red lightening bolt. Leg tag: "© 1985 Dakin, Inc., San Francisco, CA, Product of Thailand." Pharmacist in 1998 did not recognize the product name. $8-$16.

Mallinckrodt®. 9" (seated) golden brown plush bear with slightly humped back, plastic eyes and nose, small tail, floss toe separators. Tan snout, ear linings, and back paw pads. Navy blue removable T-shirt says "Mallinckrodt ®, Mallinckrodt Anesthesia Products" on the front and HiLo® tracheal Tubes// Mon-a-therm® Temperature Products" Tush tag: (crown logo) "CROWN," Tag reverse: "All new materials, synthetic fibers, Made in Taiwan." $5-$10.

Transderm Nitro. 9" seated brown bear wears maroon satin neck ribbon. A peach satin shield patch on his chest reads: "Transderm Nitro." Tush tag: "Trudy, Norwalk, CT, Made in Korea, © 1983 Trudy Toys Inc." His 5" seated white plush friend, whose shirt is part of his body, wears a red-sleeved white shirt with the name "Transderm Nitro ® (red heart) nitroglycerin." Gold hanging cord on head. Tush tag: "Made in China." The 5" bear was packaged in a clear plastic bag with printed dosage instructions. Both bears have plastic eyes and nose, and floss mouth. *Small bear courtesy of Shirley Taylor*.

Left: **Biaxin**®. 10" brown plush bear hand puppet with white snout and ear linings, plastic eyes, black velour nose, white cotton lining. Wears removable purple shirt with "BIAXIN® clarithromycin For Oral Suspension" on the chest. Side tag: "Made in China." Other animals and shirt colors were also available with this advertising message. $10-$15. The product is an antibiotic.

Below: **Kinder Care/Panadol/Tussi-Organidin.** On the left, a golden plush 10" (standing) Kinder Care's 1987 "Kinder Bear." His shirt displays the little red schoolhouse logo of the preschool facility. In the center is 3-1/2" rubber-like panda in pink shirt that says "Children's Panadol," a children's aspirin sampled to doctors' offices in 1987. On the right a brown bear, touting "Tussi-Organidin" on his shirt, is dated on his tag "1984" but was given to patients by pediatricians in 1987. *Courtesy of Ginny Kreitler.*

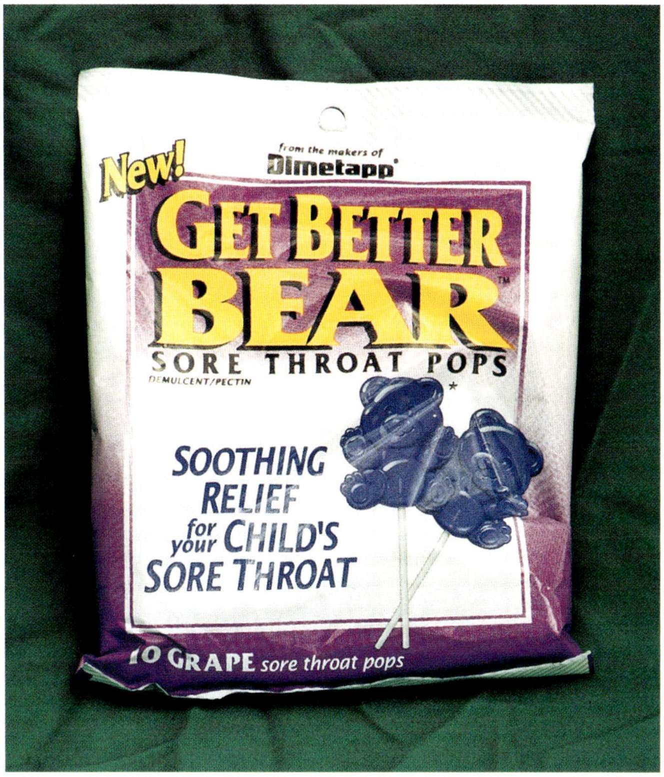

Get Better Bear. "From the makers of Dimetapp®, new "Get Better Bear" sore throat pops with demulcent and pectin. For the soothing relief for your child's sore throat, 10 grape sore throat pops-" "Unique bear design ™, © and distributed by Whitehall-Robbins Healthcare, Madison, NJ 07940." A new product introduced in October 1998 with magazine ads and TV commercials, available at drug stores for about $4.50 per package.

"Dental Ben" is the Tender Care Dental Offices spokesbear in this 1995 advertisement. Bottom right is a girl bear with "Flossy" on her dress who says "Don't forget to floss." Ad taken from a Spokane, Washington newspaper.

"United for Health, Manatee County," Florida bear advertises a 1998 health fair and coupon book to benefit the United Way of Manatee County.

Chapter 7

Bears That Help Educate

The number of organizations using bears to attract attention and help disseminate their message is growing. Seat belt, bicycle and camping safety; reforestation, saving wildlife and the environment; and "Bears Against Drugs" — all use bruins to advertise their doin's. In 1998 the Carnivore Preservation Trust introduced the first of a series of "Guardians of the Rain Forest" bears to generate donations to finance a project to care for a group of Sun Bears in Laos.

Trooper Teddy. This 10" seated brown plush bear with plastic eyes, nose, and a tail, is called "Trooper Teddy." His picture is on his removable navy blue shirt. He rides along with the regular troopers to be on hand to comfort children involved in accidents, or those hurt, or lost He can also be purchased for $15. *Courtesy of Virginia State Police Association.*

Back view of Trooper Teddy's shirt "Compliments of the Virginia State Police Association. "Tush tag: (bear logo) "ASI 62960" Tag reverse: "Made in China."

Cap'n Beware, the Safety Bear says "Play It Safe At the Beach." He's the spokesbear for Oregon State Parks. Photo is of a coloring sheet given to children at the county fair near Gold Beach, Oregon in 1994.

Copy of shield patch of the Oregon State Parks rangers printed on the reverse of Cap'n Beware, the Safety Bear coloring sheet.

B.A.D. (Bears Against Drugs). Bumper sticker calls attention to Virginia's Bears Against Drugs program of the State Police Association. It is to heighten public awareness of the drug problem. *Courtesy of Virginia State Police Association, 1998.*

Bucklebear

"Operation Bucklebear" was created in the 1980s by David Shinn, and later purchased by the Center for Injury Prevention. All related materials (tapes, books, stickers, lap puppets, etc.) are purchased from them. These materials, along with numerous programs and publications emphasizing child safety, are available by contacting:

Center for Injury Prevention
5000 Coye Drive
Stevens Point, Wisconsin 54481
(800) 344-7580

A Bucklebear ® robot Michigan trooper driving his own official patrol car. He's a very attention getting promotional device. *Photo courtesy of the Center for Injury Prevention.*

"Bucklebear"® lap puppet being used to instruct school children in the necessity of buckling seat belts, wearing helmets; and walking, riding, cycling safely. The national program, called "Operation Bucklebear," is sponsored by the Center for Injury Prevention, headquartered in Stevens Point, Wisconsin. The Bucklebear ® pictured is being used by the Lee County (Florida) Medical Society Alliance Foundation. A training video, "The Bucklebear Lap Puppet Presenter Training Program" was developed for the San Antonio Safe Kids Coalition. The lap puppet is one of four types of Bucklebears ® used to educate the public. *Photo courtesy of the Center for Injury Prevention.*

The third type of Bucklebear ® is the person-sized costume. This one is delivering a basketful of 7" x 7-1/2" soft cotton printed Bucklebears ®. *Photo courtesy of the Center for Injury Prevention.*

These little 7" softly stuffed Bucklebear ® Companion bears are furnished to Bucklebear ® program sponsors for use in a number of ways including instruction, and gifts to students or traumatized children. *Bears courtesy of the Center for Injury Prevention.*

"Bucklebear's ® Rules for Young Walkers" and "Walking with Bucklebear ®, A story just for you" are two of the instructional books used in the Bucklebear ® program. Eight titles are available in Spanish. *Courtesy of the Center for Injury Prevention.*

"Riding with Bucklebear ®, A story for young passengers" and "Bucklebear's ® Rules for Cycling" are two more instructional materials. Others include birthday puzzle cards (a personal birthday greeting from Bucklebear ®), practice bears (demonstrating the proper use of safety seat), safety strobe lights (to wear on clothing at night), books, stickers, and felt play kits. *Courtesy of the Center for Injury Prevention.*

"Biking with Bucklebear ®" and "Helmet Safe with Bucklebear ®" are two more books from the Bucklebear ® program. Bike safety helmets are also available from the program. *Courtesy of the Center for Injury Prevention.*

Two additional titles are "Bucklebear ® Meets the Airbags" and "The Bucklebear ® Good Passenger Book." *Courtesy of the Center for Injury Prevention.*

Tree Bear

Tree Bear — the spokesbear for better forest management — was the brain child of Harry Rossoll, who also "fathered" Smokey Bear. The *Tree Bear Book*, story by June A. Bradlaw (Rossoll's niece), was illustrated by Mr. Rossoll (who passed away in March 1999). In 1996-97 *The Woodland Catalog* introduced T-shirts with the Tree Bear logo. Their '97-'98 catalog offered a Tree Bear hat as well.

Mr. Harry Rossoll, one of the artists who conceived Smokey Bear. He drew more than 1,000 "Smokey Says" cartoons for the USFS. In this 1998 photo, he's holding a 15" Smokey Bear by Three Bears Inc. © 1985, and his new creation 19" "Tree Bear." (Raggedy Ann fans will be interested to know that, in 1929, Mr. Rossoll attended art school in New York City with his lifelong friend Worth Gruelle.) *Photo by Shane Keating, courtesy of Harry Rossoll and Tom & Joni Gruelle Wannamaker.*

Tree Bear. Mr. Rossoll's drawing of Tree Bear and the Tree Bear logo on a book mark which reminds "Good things come from Trees." On the reverse is the message "Visit Oklahoma Forest Heritage Center in Beavers Bend Resort Park, Museum Art Gallery, History in Dioramas, Paintings, Pioneer Cabin, Memorabilia, Nature Tree Trail, Center Gift Shop." *Courtesy of Harry Rossoll.*

19" Tree Bear, created by artist Harry Rossoll, is the newest in forest protectors. Tree Bear, who is "manly in a sensitive, intelligent way," wears wire rimmed glasses, a ball cap, green jacket and pants, and carries a dibble bar, a tree planting tool. His message is that "good things come from trees" and "with proper stewardship of private land, we can have our forests and wood products, too." The Oklahoma Forest Heritage Center and the National Woodland Owner' s Association have adopted the Tree Bear symbol. T-shirts, hats, and bookmarks with Tree Bear's picture are available. Tree Bear attended the Atlanta Olympics and is the subject of a book, by Mr. Rossoll's niece, now awaiting publication. *Photo by Shane Keating, courtesy of Harry Rossoll and Tom & Joni Gruelle Wannamaker.*

Timbear. The front cover of Timbear's activity workbook "Welcome to Timbear's Unibearsity, Remember Smart People Say No to Bad Drugs." On back cover "© 1989 O.F. Hall, Distributed by Common Sense, Inc., 1461 Meadowlark Lane, Sweet Home, OR 97386" Their message: "Trees are a renewable resource, just like the crops that our nation's farmers grow to provide us with food. Trees are plants that are grown and harvested that we may have warm homes, paper, pencils, clothing and even medicines such as taxol for cancer patients. These are just a few of the products that come from our forests. We would not be provided with these products without the wise harvesting and replanting of trees." A costumed Timbear visited schools. Workbooks and recordings were supplied to teachers and children's organizations. The author's research did not discover whether this program is still operating.

World Wildlife Fund

5" seated black and white plush Panda with green neck bow. Tush tag: "World Wildlife Fund, © 1988 Determined Productions Inc, San Francisco, CA, Product of Korea." Paper pamphlet tag: "Wendy's ®, World Wildlife Fund, Plush Toy, (panda figure) © WWF, Help Save Us! ™" Inside the tag: "Wendy's is proud to support the efforts of World Wildlife Fund to protect the world's endangered animals and the wild lands where they live." Inside are 11 pages telling about the Giant Panda. A 14 page book, *All About Giant Pandas*, © 1986 WWF, © 1988 Wendy's, was also available during the promotion. Panda with paper tag and book: $10-$15.

6" seated gray plush Koala with green neck bow. Tush tag is the same as Panda's. Paper pamphlet tag tells about Koalas. Accompanying Wendy/World Wildlife book is called *All About Koalas*. Koala with paper tag and book: $10-$15.

6" seated plush Snow Leopard and 6" standing Tiger with their accompanying Wendy/World Wildlife Fund books. Missing their paper tags. $8-$12 each with book.

5" (seated) Panda with plastic eyes, plush nose, floss mouth. He holds a sealed bottle of "Naturistics® Sea-Splash Cologne" made with oils of lime, orange, and Ylang Ylang. © 1998 Del Laboratories, Farmingdale, NY. His paper ear tag says "Endangered Species Naturistics® Fragrance Collectibles" On reverse: "Natural Ingredients, Not Tested on Animals." Retail price: $3.99.

5-1/2" glass from Burger Chef's "Endangered Species, 1978 Collector's Series, The Giant Panda" and a description of the Panda's habitat. Also says "World Wildlife Fund." $2-$8.

4" jam jars from Welch's "Endangered Species Collection," both contained concord grape jam. They are marked "Welch's & World Wildlife Fund." Giant Panda is listed as #1 and Spectacled Bear as #10. The metal lids say "© 1994 Welch's." $2-$8 each.

Back view of Welch's 1994 "Endangered Species" jam jars for World Wildlife Fund.

A 1998 Sunday supplement ad says "Help Save Me with New Johnson's Endangered Species" shampoo, body wash, conditioner products. The Giant Panda is on the front of the green shampoo bottle. "Free 3-D Collector Cards with purchase." "WWF" panda figure at bottom of ad, along with the address to join.

The Nature Conservancy. 10" seated shaggy brown plush bear, "Wildlife" button added by owner. This was a 1991 Warner-Lambert Co. promotion called "Help Save Our Wildlife." The price was $9.95 plus 1 proof-of-purchase from Listerine, Listermint, or Efferdent. Warner-Lambert donated 30 cents to The Nature Conservancy for each bear purchased. Tag: "Animal Fair, Eden Valley, MN." *Courtesy of Jean Laughery, Photo by Vivian L. Gery.*

National Park Foundation. Ad for Mott's apple juice or sauce, offering a 9" brown grizzly bear (or a green sea turtle, or Florida panther) for 12 Mott's proof-of-purchase apple symbols and $1 shipping, or for $6.99 and 2 proofs-of-purchase. "Mott's will make a contribution to the National Park Foundation for each animal ordered." Offer expired February 1, 1994.

Earth Day. A 1994 ad for Arm & Hammer products suggests: "Take the Arm & Hammer ® 'Environmental Quotient' Test—it's an important part of 'Doing our Share for Clean Water and Air.' The Arm & Hammer® family of products and the National Fish and Wildlife Foundation are committed to creating new environmental education programs — that's why it's important for you to take our E.Q. Test so we'll have a better idea of what you need to know."
A $5,000 scholarship or trip to Yellowstone National Park were offered in a drawing. A brown bear delivers the message.

Chapter 8
Tourist Bears

What souvenir would a bear collector wish for from a vacation, trip, or attraction? A bear, of course! The tourist bears shown here are a minor sampling of the many bears available, from such widely separated places as Chicago, the Great Smokies, Hawaii, Busch Gardens, Knott's Berry Farm, Cordova Mall, Universal Studios, and the S. S. Constitution.

Places

Alcatraz Penitentiary. 14-1/2" light brown bear dressed in his prison garb. His prison number, #137066, is printed on his suit front (part of his body); his hat identifies him as "Alcatraz Penitentiary Bear." Red neck ribbon, black plastic eyes/nose, white feet, white snout and ear linings. Tag: "1985." *Courtesy of Ginny Kreitler.*

Atlanta. 8" seated all white plush bear with tail, plastic eyes and brown velour nose. Wears removable red shirt with "I (heart) Atlanta" machine embroidered in white. Tush tag: "Made in Korea." $5-$10.

Cape Canaveral. 21" dark brown plush bear, "Cub CanaBEARal" in space suit with "Moon Rock" and "Swiss Cheese" in his side pockets. Tag: "North American Bear Co, 1984" *Courtesy of Bonnie and Larry Vaughan.*

Chicago. 6" seated cinnamon brown bear with tail, cream snout, plastic eyes, black floss nose and mouth, carries a burlap bag. His orange shirt saying "I Love Chicago" is part of his body. Woven leg tag: "© R. Dakin, 1978, San Francisco, CA, Product of Korea." $5-$10.

Colorado. 5" seated gray and white plush panda with gray tail, black plush eye surrounds, blue plastic eyes, black velour nose. His 1-1/2" button says "Colorado" in white against purple mountains. Plastic tag in ear indicates he had an ear tag. Woven leg tag: "© 1985 SWIB, Lisle, Illinois, Made in Korea." $4-$8.

Cordova Mall. 6" seated black and white plush panda, no tail, with 2-1/2" hanging loop on head. Red-sleeved white shirt says in red: "Cordova Mall" (located in Pensacola, Florida). Tag on shirt back: "Made in Philippines." Tush tag front: a yellow bear logo and washing instructions. Tag back: "It's All Greek To Me" [that's the company name], Eton Avenue, Canoga Park, CA, Made in Philippines." $4-$8.

Daytona Beach. 5" seated light gray plush koala, white ear tufts, snout, and back paw pads, plastic eyes, black plastic nose, raised arms. His white shirt with red trim at neckline and cuffs says "I (red heart) Daytona Beach" (Florida). Leg tag: "Non-toxic and washable, Made in Korea." $4-$8.

Deep Creek Lake. 10" seated black and white plush panda with black tail, plastic eyes, black velour nose. Wears removable red shirt with a white sailboat and "Deep Creek Lake, Maryland" painted on the front. Tush tag: bear logo, "ASI —560, Made in Indonesia." Has original price tag from "The Trading Post, 301-387-5553" $12.99.

Florida. 9" beige plush jointed (arms/legs) bear with no tags. Wears white top with red trim and "I (red heart) Florida. Two red buttons on pleats of shirt back. Red ribbon rose and red and green ribbon streamers between her ears. Tan felt paw pads, plastic eyes, floss nose, mouth, and paw stitching. No tags. Heavy white glue is on the back of her neck so she may have been attached to something. $5-$8.

Hawaii. 18" Leilani souvenir bear, by Robert Raikes, a limited edition of 250, only available to Robert Raikes Collectors Club members at their September 1994 convention on Maui. She has the typical Raikes carved wooden face, wears a bra top, grass skirt, both flower and shell leiș, and wears a flower by her ear (to indicate she's single?). Price unavailable.

Myrtle Beach. 11" seated beige plush bear, black plastic nose, dime-sized plastic eyes, floss smile, white snout, ear linings, and paw pads. The white satin shirt front says "Myrtle Beach" with a sail boat inside a circle. Shirt is part of the body. Tush tag: "Imported by Strand Import, Myrtle Beach, S.C. 29577, All new material, Made in China." $6-$12.

The Pines. 5-1/2" standing brown plush bear, unjointed, with tan ears and snout, plastic eyes, brown plastic nose, red felt tongue, red neck ribbon. Wears removable white tank top with a red circle of trees and "The Pines." No state or locality is given, purchased in Florida. Leg tag: "Steven Smith © Stuffed Animals Inc., Brooklyn, NY, Made in Korea." $4-$8.

San Francisco. 10" seated brown plush bear with white snout, plastic eyes, plastic nose, floss mouth. His ribbed navy blue pants and white shirt with navy/white striped sleeves are part of his body. Shirt says "I Love (red heart) San Francisco" in navy blue. He has a cub bear look. Tush tag: "Made in Korea, acrylic fiber." $5-$10.

Great Smoky Mountains. On the left 9" standing black short-pile plush bear, red felt tongue, white ear linings, snout, shirt (part of body). Shirt has stick-on letters that spell out "I (red heart) The Smokies." No tags. Soft like a baby's toy. Bear is missing his plastic nose. On the right 10" standing black shaggy plush bear with tan snout, paw pads, and ear linings. Plastic eyes and nose. Wears removable white shirt with Velcro® back fastening. Depicted on the shirt is a black bear on all fours with "Great Smoky Mts." printed in red. Leg tag: "Fairway Mfg Co, St Louis, MO." 9": $3-$6 as is; 10": $6-$10.

Texas. "Don't mess with Texas" is the anti-litter slogan for the State. This 12" standing golden plush bear wears a shirt (part of his body) with that warning. His red vest is his body in the back and seam-stitched red cotton in the front. His stuffed yellow flannel derby (What? No 10 gallon Stetson?) is perched just above his inquisitive oval plastic eyes. White snout, ear linings, and back paw pads, black plastic nose, floss mouth. Leg tag: "Made in China, © 1991 P.M.I. Toys and Novelties, San Antonio, Texas." $8-$12.

Texas. 9" seated silky shaggy brown plush bear, with sheared tummy, plastic eyes and receding plastic nose, rust colored ribbon neck bow. Paper tag: "Little Blanco Inn, Twin Sisters, Texas" in light blue. Tag appears homemade. Tush tag: "Made in Taiwan." His face resembles an owl. $5-$10.

Big Bear Lake. 3" tall cast metal bear with blue enamel shield depicting a tree, bear, and "Big Bear Lake, Calif." "Japan" printed on base in back. Green felt on bottom. $3-$5. *Courtesy of Robin's Collectibles*.

Cape Cod/Atlantic City. Two ceramic tourist bears. The 3" golden molded ceramic bear with red bow tie and "I (heart) Cape Cod" is a tiny bud vase. Paper sticker tag on bottom says "by Karol Western, Los Angeles, California, Made in Taiwan." The 3-1/2" brown "I (heart) Atlantic City" bear is a hollow figurine. Paper sticker tag on bottom says "Made in Taiwan." $3-$5 each.

Attractions

Cass Scenic Railroad, Cass, West Virginia. A pair of plush railroad engineer bears seated on a train bench between train rides. Large chubby engineer bear is 16" tall and 10" wide. Small bear is 9" tall and 8" wide. Their clothes appear to be part of their bodies. Overalls labels say: "Cass Scenic Railroad, Cass, West Virginia." Tags read: "Fairway Mfg Co, Acrylic Pile Stuffing Polyester, Made in China." *Courtesy of Greg and Maryam Gerardi.*

Busch Gardens. 7" seated gray koala bear with black felt toes, black plastic nose, plastic eyes, white tummy, ear tufts, and eye surrounds. Velcro® strip on arms allows him to hug something. Woven tush tag: "Busch Gardens ®, Tampa, Florida, Made in Korea." $5-$10

Cheers. 13" seated white plush bear, plastic eyes and plastic nose with nostrils indented. The message on his apron invites us to "Meet Me In Cheers ™ © 1992 Par. Pic." (Paramount Pictures) Apron trim and ties are black. Tush tag missing. $7-$15.

Circus Circus. 11" seated all white plush bear with 2" tail holds a 4-1/2" x 4" stuffed red heart saying "Circus ® Circus" in white. Plastic eyes and nose, 8" leg spread. Tush tag: "Softouch Toys, California, Made in Korea."$5-$10.

Chicago Zoo. A family of molded brown bears go exploring. The two smallest bears (1-1/2" tall x 3" long) have, in raised lettering, on their sides "Chicago's New Zoo, Brookfield, Ill." Mama bear is 2-1/2" tall x 5-1/2" long. Circa 1930s. *Courtesy of Nancy Vanselow, Verner A. Swanson collection.*

Circus Circus. 10" standing beige plush bear with rust snout and ear linings, plastic eyes. He wears a removable judo "gi" and cord belt. No tail. Tush tag: "Circus Circus, Las Vegas, Nev., Made in China." $5-$10.

Fiesta Texas. 15" seated bright gold plush bear in black body shirt that advertises "Fiesta Texas, San Antonio" below a white Lone Star. Cuffs and belt are gold lame, back paw pads are black plush. Black velour ear linings, black plastic gumdrop sized nose, plastic eyes, raised arms, firmly stuffed body, cute crooked floss smile. Leg tag: "P.M.I. International, San Antonio, Texas, Shell Made in China, © 1991." $8-$10.

Circus Circus. 7" seated white plush bear with orange arms, footpads, and ear linings has black plastic nose, and red felt tongue. This "cool" tourist bear wears plastic sunglasses and a blue bow. Tag reads: "Circus Circus, Las Vegas, Reno, Made in China, Contents Polyester." $5-$8.

Knott's Berry Farm. 9" standing white plush bear wearing red plush overalls and red flannel hat, pink plastic nose, plastic eyes. Red grosgrain ribbon shoulder straps cross in back, two red plastic fake buttons on overalls front. Tush tag: "Knott's Berry Farm, Buena Park, California, Handcrafted in (country blurred)" Strawberry and basket not original with bear. $5-$8.

Ringling Bros. 6-1/2" seated brown plush circus bear with 5-1/2" black hanging loop on head. White plush bib, dark brown plush eyebrows, brown tail, cream ear linings, snout, and back paw pads, plastic eyes and tiny black plastic nose, floss mouth. Velcro® strips on each front paw don't stick together. His accessory unknown. Tush tag: "© 1983 Ringling Bros. - Barnum & Bailey Combined Shows Inc., Made in Korea." Plastic circus wagon is not original with bear. $5-$10.

Opryland. This pair of 13" white plush bears (head and paws only) have plastic eyes and nose and a red felt tongue. Their light pink satiny suits have a pattern of colorful splashes and the word "Opryland" (in Nashville, Tennessee) in script. Although they come from the Country Music Capitol, they are not musical bears, just very huggable. Their tush tags read: "Roni Toy Inc." in blue script on one side and on the reverse: "© Roni Toy Inc 1987, Jersey City, New Jersey, Made in China." $5-$8 each.

Silver Dollar City/ Spring Mill State Park/ St. Louis Union Station. On the left brown plush bear in white shirt is from Silver Dollar City amusement park in Missouri, purchased in 1985. The 9" bear in the middle hails from Spring Mill State Park, Mitchell, Indiana. He has the same face on his front and back. On the right, in a red and white engineer's cap and red polka dot neckerchief, is the bear representing St. Louis Union Station, an historic train station converted to a posh shopping center. Purchased at the train station gift shop in 1987. *Courtesy of Ginny Kreitler.*

Sea World. Advertisement catches a costumed sailor bear from Sea World posing for a clothing sale promotion in 1997. Sea World's mug and sipper bottle show a seal wearing this outfit.

Six Flags. 11" seated beige plush bear wears a body shirt inviting us to "Six Flags" amusement parks. Tush tag: "Logo Bear, America Wego Inc., © 1982, Made in Korea." Plastic eyes, brown velour nose. Flag not original to bear. (Six Flags also sold 4-1/2" ceramic souvenir banks shaped like bears with "Six Flags, Texas" medallions on their tummies. Costumed bears entertained park visitors.) $5-$10.

S.S. Constitution. 8" seated all white plush bear with tail wears removable red shirt with "I (white heart) S.S. Constitution" machine embroidered in white across the front. Tush tag: "Preferred Services Ltd,, New York, NY, Made in Korea." $4-$10.

Toytown USA, East Aurora, NY. 12-1/2" standing brown bear, replica of 1920 Classic Teddybar by Steiff wears a satin sash identifying him as a souvenir of "Toyfest '97." This is an annual event in the hometown of Fisher-Price toys. *Courtesy of Tom and Joni Gruelle Wannamaker.*

Universal Studios®. 7" seated purple plush bear wears a removable white T-shirt with a design of a circle around a movie camera and the words "Universal Studios ®" Plastic eyes and nose. Tush tag: "Made in China." $5-$10.

Chapter 9
Those Foreign Fellows

In addition to domestic tourist bears, foreign bears are often found, especially those from Berlin, Germany and Bern, Switzerland. The city emblem for each locality is a bear.

Berlin's black bear adorns the city flag of white with red bands at top and bottom. On the state flag the bear appears on a crowned shield — the City's Arms — with a golden crown, red claws and tongue, on a white background.

Bern means bear. It was founded in 1101 by a duke whom legend says built the city in gratitude to heaven for his surviving an attack by bears while he was hunting. Bears are everywhere in Bern. The canton's Coat of Arms, "red with a yellow diagonal charged with a black bear," is used on their canton flag. Bears are among the figures which, since 1530, have emerged hourly from the astronomic clock tower. The Zahringer fountain is topped by a bear in armor, the city's heraldic device. A famous Bern landmark is the bear pit where live bears have been on display since 1513.

Happily, bears immigrate from other corners of the globe, as well. A newly heard about (but not new) foreign bear is Great Britain's comic strip bear "Super Ted," a superhero complete with cape. "Homegrown" but having a definite foreign flair are the new Hansel and Gretel bears by Robert Raikes.

Berlin. 5" black and white bear with white neck ribbon with red edges and "Berliner Bar" spelled out in black script. Plastic eyes, red felt tongue, 2" inch red cord loop stitched to head. Tush tag: "SA 595, Made in China." $10-$15.

Berlin. 4-1/2" gold bear with jointed arms and legs, wearing 1" gold foil crown and silky fringed scarf tied over his shoulder. Scarf has an embroidered bear and "Berlin." Plastic eyes and tongue, stitched nose and mouth, no tags. *Courtesy of Peggy Monahan.*

Berlin. Gold jointed bear wearing gold foil crown, red neck bow, and "Berliner Bar" ribbon around his waist. Berlin bear on shield pin on his chest, and the front of his paper ear tag. *Courtesy of Nancy Vanselow.*

Berlin. 12" brown plush bear with beige muzzle, ear linings, and paw pads, wearing a tiny red crown and a banner in celebration of the 750th anniversary of Berlin. The banner says: "1237-1987, 750" with a sketch of the Red (brick) City Hall, which was East Berlin's city hall and now serves as the city hall for the unified city. Plastic eyes and nose, floss mouth. *Courtesy of Greg Gerardi.*

East Berlin. A cute little 12" white lambs-wool like plush Communist Cossack bear with a brown muzzle and ear linings. Dressed in black plush hat, black pants, red shirt with white cord belt. Plastic eyes, nose, and red felt mouth. Purchased in East Berlin before the Wall came down. *Courtesy of Greg Gerardi.*

Australia. 7" brownish gray plush Koala bear with white ears and plastic nose, wears a light green neck ribbon. Woven leg tag reads: "Downunda Souvenirs P/ L, Gosford, NSW [New South Wales] 2250, Australia." Tag reverse: "All new materials, Synthetic Fibers, Made in Australia." $5-$8.

Australia. I explained to this 'Roo that this book is about bears, but she reminded me I have an Australian aunt, and she wouldn't take "No" for an answer. The 8" seated cinnamon brown plush Mama Kangaroo, with baby Joey in her white pouch, wears a red neck ribbon, which says "Australia" in gold. Paper tag is a replica of the Australian flag. Tush tag: A ram's head logo ™, "Carlington of Australia" and a telephone number. Tag reverse:" Australian designed, Made in China." *Courtesy of Dr. Muriel Hoffman.*

Bahamas. 8" seated gray plush bear with plastic eyes and nose, and wearing a removable red sweatshirt with a black palm tree and "Bahamas" on the front. Tush tag: "Made in China." $4-$8.

Botswana. 15" gray looped wool bear with dark gray eyes, nose, paw pads, and ear linings. Tag sewn on bottom "Handwoven, Tiro Ya Diatza, Lobatse-Botswana." Paper tag: "© 1984 Zakanaka, Inc." *Courtesy of Nancyann Eckhart.*

Canada. 10" brown plush bear in red ribbed short pants, and white shirt with candy-cane striped sleeves (all part of body). Shirt says "I Love (red maple leaf) Canada" in blue. White snout, amber plastic eyes, brown plastic nose, floss mouth. Tush tag (in English and French): "Imported by Dan Dee Imports, Made in Korea." $5-$10.

Canada. "Life" Brand advertising bear for the Shoppers Drug Mart stores made of good quality, two tone plush. Note his eyebrows and "cowlick" of hair between his ears. He is a familiar emblem on Canadian shopper's Drug Mart baby products. Original (pre-1992) purchase price: $8.99 (Canadian). Mini plastic bear is also the "Life" bear. They are no longer available. *Courtesy of Jacqueline Wilson, Photo by Russ Wilson.*

Canada. "Punkinhead" is Eaton department store's comical mascot. The bear was issued by Merrythought in the late 1940s and discontinued in 1957. Punkinhead reappeared in the 1970s as a reissued bear (this time in synthetic fabric), but did not regain popularity. He was again reissued in the 1990s with an updated version of the earlier mascot. None of the later bears became as popular as the original character. The 10" "Baby Punkinhead" bear pictured dates to 1949. He is mohair with glass eyes, velveteen feet, felt pads on front paws, excelsior-stuffed, and wears his original blue felt shorts. Shorts could be blue, yellow, green, or red. "Punkinhead" came in sizes up to 25". Merrythought recently issued an 8" fully jointed mohair, limited edition of 1000, look-alike bear introduced in 1957 that Queen Elizabeth II called "Cheeky." The 1998 value of a 20" 1960s Punkinhead was $1,500 and up. *Courtesy of Jacqueline Wilson, Photo by Russ Wilson, pricing by Dee Hockenberry.*

Canada. 14" seated beige plush "Zeddy" teddy bear (with tail) is an advertising bear for Zeller's Stores in Canada. This is the first Zeddy ever made. He wears a removable white shirt with Velcro® back closing. Note his name on his left paw, and the white highlight dots on his plastic eyes. Tush tag: in English and French "Made in Korea." Other versions of Zeddy exist. There are many products (i.e. coloring books) relating to Zeddy. *Courtesy of Jacqueline Wilson, Photo by Russ Wilson.*

Canada. A label from a Canadian Kraft (smooth) peanut butter jar written in English and French. The twin bears were also made as stuffed animals. *Courtesy of Kelly Catto Gerardi.*

Germany. Steiff traveler bear dressed in *lederhosen* and red and white checked shirt. His chest is covered with pins from all of the towns he has visited. (A European traveling custom, collect a pin from each town you visit and display them on your hat.) Leather suitcase is not original to him. *Courtesy of Nancy Vanselow.*

Germany. Black Forest limited edition (500 each) mohair bears by Hermann. 17" boy and 16-1/2" girl are dressed in black velveteen Alpine outfits. They are fully jointed, stuffed with excelsior, and contain growlers. Paws are embroidered with name and edition number. He wears a cuckoo clock hatpin on his lapel and carries a wooden clock ornament. Red pompoms top her hat. 1998 issue price: $200 each.

Germany. The cover of a children's activity book in German starring "Bussi Bar" (busy bear). $2-$5.

Great Britain. Two London landmark bears. On the right is 10" "Harry Heathrow" (airport) bear in yellow shirt showing his plane and name. The 11" Harrods department store doorman was made by Merrythought of England. *Courtesy of Dee Domroe.*

Great Britain. 16-1/2" standing, Queen's Guardsman His hat with blue plume, shirt, gloves, and pants are all plush and a part of his body. He's stiffly stuffed so maintains his military bearing. Amber plastic eyes, black nose with nostril indentations, and gold cord chin strap. The British flag on his belt is a paper sticker. No tags. The oversized London pencil is not original to him. $10-$15.

Great Britain. Beanie Baby "Brittania," a European exclusive, date of birth 12/15/97. Inside her Ty paper folder ear tag: "Brittania the bear will sail the sea, So she can be with you and me, She's always sure to catch the tide, And wear the Union flag with pride." Brown with red ribbon neck bow and the British "Union Jack" embroidered on her right breast. A real cutie with a 1998 valuation of $525.00. *Courtesy of L. Victor Desguin.*

Great Britain. Advertisement for golden "Ben the London Bear" by Planet Plush ™, ©1999 Royal Boca Publishing Inc., Planet Plush trademark owned by Palm Investments Limited. Limited edition of 36,000, bowler hat not included, no size given in the ad. Brown bear with fabric timepiece sewn to his chest. Price unavailable.

Great Britain. Teddy Tum Tum Toy Company - A 12" x 16-1/2" metal sign advertising "The Teddy Tum Tum Toy Company, London, England" shows a boy and girl bear sitting amongst toys in the nursery. Found in Sanford, North Carolina, 1998. $15-$25.

Holland. 9" (seated) brown plush bear with beige snout, ear linings, and back paw pads, plastic eyes and nose, and floss mouth. White removable T-shirt says "Hard Rock ® Café, Amsterdam." One tush tag: "Hard Rock Café, Amsterdam" Tag reverse: "Specially Made for Hard Rock Café, Amsterdam, Made in China." Second tag "CE, UTS BV WEESP, Holland." His doll companion is dressed in the wooden shoes and ethnic costume of the region. $5-$15.

Hong Kong. 17" Tsingtao Beer Bear, is made of jute and wears a khaki two-piece Communist uniform with 3 brass buttons, a cap with yellow, red, and black trim, and flannel shoes that tie. His paper tag says: "Ode to Little China Hands, Pick me up, give me a squeeze, There is someone at home I'm sure to please. I'm Tsingtao Bear, I'm really cute (it's because I'm made of ruff tuff jute). In the middle kingdom we're a household word, and we like a beer, we know you've heard. A "Little China Hand" is what you need, to do a good friend a deed. For when next remembered that famous brew, a Tsingtao Bear will be remembered too!" *Courtesy of Nancy Harmon*.

New Zealand. A beige teddy by Harrison's ("Toys with a Heart") in a red shirt with "Thomas Cook" (bank, travelers checks, and travel tours/arrangements) on the right side. Since 1981 the Auckland, New Zealand firm Harrison's has been making bears to promote New Zealand products from department stores, to diapers, to fabric softeners. Prices unknown. They sell through their catalog.

Japan. 8-1/2" white headed plush bear with brown ears, paws and brown 2-1/2" tail. He's dressed in satin groom's outfit of striped pants, removable jacket, leatherette shoes, and a top hat stitched to his head. His triangle shaped paper neck tag says "Bridal Party" (also picturing a bride). The leg tag in English says "Amuse ®" "For premium use only." The rest of the tag is in Japanese. $10-$15.

U.S.S.R. Strange little 8" standing Russian bear. His red flannel shirt says "University of Moscow" and is part of his body. His long black head hair reveals a brown leatherette bald spot. Tush tag: "Ace Novelty Co. Inc." Tag reverse: "© Ace Novelty Co Inc, Los Angeles-Chicago-Seattle, Made in China." $5-$10.

Chapter 10

Beary Helpful Information

Selection

Rule Number One: buy only those bears you love and want to share your home space with (unless you are buying for resale or just can't resist the price, thus obtaining bears inexpensively for trading purposes). While gathering information for this book, I bought nearly every advertising bear I saw. Some will remain in residence. Others will be adopted out to good homes.

Selection criteria differs for each collector, whether for a general collection or one or more of the following categories:

- High quality limited editions
- Specific maker
- Specific artist/designer
- Product bears
- One specific product
- Tourist bears, domestic or foreign
- Sports bears or
- One specific team
- Hobbies: golf, tennis, skating, gardening
- Specific types: Panda, koala, different colors, fur, dressed, undressed
- Specific size, for example miniatures
- Specific characters: Yogi, Smokey, Paddington, Pooh, Berenstain, Snuggle
- Celebrity bears
- Storybook bears
- Corporate tags
- Message bears (Happy Birthday, I Love You, etc.)
- Bears that demand to be a part of your family

Identification

I recall a fashion article of the 1950s suggesting that we drape our coat, jacket or sweater over the chairback at a restaurant in order to show off its label. The writer lamented it was the only way to let the expensive maker label be seen. Fifty years later it is nearly impossible to find a pair of jeans or sneakers, a shirt, T-shirt or hat that does NOT proclaim the product or designer's logo or name in read-across-the-room sized letters.

When hunting for collectible advertising bears, remember that not all bears will have logos emblazoned conspicuously on their chest. Some, like the Elizabeth Arden bear, have only discreet sewn-in seam tags.

Some bears are marked in several places, others in only one place. You'll find advertising information on:

- Paper tags
- Plastic tags
- Body tags
- Ear buttons
- Chest buttons
- T-shirts
- Neck ribbons
- Body sashes
- Hats (often baseball or knitted caps)
- Clothes (jeans, sweater, overalls, dress, shirt, pocket, belt)
- Name embroidered or stenciled on a foot
- Name on a patch on the backside
- A product (Coke bottle, Hershey's bar) the bear is holding
- A team pennant the bear is holding
- Mark on neck if vinyl head
- Mark on bottom if bear is porcelain or resin

If you find a bear you think is a duplicate, check its tag, it may have been made by a different company, have a different date, or have been produced in another country. Some tags, like those of Gund and R. Dakin, will conveniently give copyright dates, others are undated and require research on your part. For example, undated Gund bears can be sorted out according to the address shown on the tags: From 1940 to 1956 the address was New York City. From 1956 to 1973 it was Suydam Street, Brooklyn. From 1972 to 1987 their location was Ethel Road in Edison, New Jersey; the address since 1987 has been Runyons Lane, Edison.

Price Determinations

In addition to condition of the bear and popularity of the product, several other factors affect the price/value of an advertising bear:

Prices will be HIGHER if:

- It is MIB (mint in box), MIP (mint in package), NRFB (never removed from the box)
- The company is no longer in business
- The product is no longer available
- All tags: body, paper, plastic, are intact
- All clothes and accessories are present

- o It is accompanied by the original ad or premium offer
- o In sports, if the uniforms or hometowns have changed or their names or mascots are no longer politically "correct" (e.g. Braves, Chiefs, Indians, Redskins, Blackhawks)
- o It is a limited edition
- o It is made by a top-of-the-line company
- o It is of superior quality
- o It is made of mohair and has glass eyes.
- o It is an older bear (1890s through 1960s) Pre 1945 is considered antique.
- o It was available for a very short time
- o It is part of a package with dated ads picturing the bear
- o The bear has a particularly attractive or appealing outfit or appearance

The price generally will be LESS if:

- o Identifying T-shirt or tags are missing
- o The only identification is a paper tag
- o The only identification is an undated body tag
- o The product or service is not well known
- o Interest is strictly regional
- o Department store bears tend to be less pricey on the secondary market than product bears

Of course, bear and advertising collectors have, for years, been picking up pre-owned advertising bears at garage sales, thrift shops, and flea markets for extremely reasonable prices: 25 cents to $5. Antique shops tagged them at $5 to $15. But with the advent of "bear fever," this has escalated to $15 to $35. The diversity of advertising bears available is encouraging and challenging to the collector.

Purchase Resources

If you'd like to buy some advertising bears, or if you just want to dream and drool over them, send for catalogs from these companies:

- o American Originals, PO Box 85098, Richmond, VA 23285-5098 (brand name gear)
- o L.L. Bean Inc., Casco St, Freeport, ME 04033
- o bear-in-mind, inc., 53 Bradford St, W. Concord, MA 01742 (since 1978)
- o The Blessed Companion Bear Co, 28 Mountain View Ave, San Rafael, CA 94901
- o Harriet Carter ®, Dept 38, North Wales, PA 19455 (NFL cheerleader bear)
- o Coca-Cola™ Catalog, 2515 E. 43rd St, PO Box 182264, Chattanooga, TN 37422
- o Colorful Images, 2910 Colorful Ave, Longmont, CO 80504-6214 (Boyds & other bears)
- o Cooperstown Bears, 1275 Busch Parkway, Buffalo Grove, IL 60089
- o Douglas Cuddle Toys, Box D, Keene, NH 05431-0716
- o Gimbel & Sons Country Store ®, PO Box 57, Boothbay Harbor, ME 04538-0057
- o Lands' End, Inc., One Lands' End Road, Dodgeville, WI 53595-0001
- o The Lighter Side™, Co, PO Box 25600, Bradenton, FL, 34206-5600 (since 1914)
- o Manny's Baseball Land, PO Box 1632, Secaucus, NJ 07096-1632 (official catalog of major league baseball)
- o North American Bear Co, 401 N. Wabash, Suite 500, Chicago, IL 60511
- o 1-800 Pro Team, PO Box 1622, Secaucus, NJ 07096-1622 (NHL & NFL bears)
- o Tender Heart Treasures, Ltd., 10525 J St., Omaha, NE 68127-1090, 1-800-443-1367 (Lots of bears.)
- o West-Tex Collectibles, PO Box 1508345, Arlington, TX 76015-6835, (advertising collectibles including Texaco bears)
- o Woodland Enterprises, 310 N. Main St, Moscow, ID 81841 (Smokey Bear & Tree Bear items)
- o Carol Wright Gifts®, PO Box 8502, Lincoln, NE 68544 (Team NFL etc)

Bear collector magazine ads, newspaper ad inserts, and grocery store packaging are still viable avenues for obtaining advertising bears and other advertising items. Be on the lookout for these send-away sources.

Addresses of Interest

Publications

- o *Beans & Bears!* (monthly magazine), PO Box 569, Dubuque, IA 52004-9864.
- o *Hot Foot Teddy Newsletter*, PO Box 1416, Westwood, CA 96137 (Qtrly, $20/yr, Smokey Bear information) Website: http\\www.smokey-ouly.com (a dash, not an underline and all lower case letters)
- o *Joy of Collecting* (bi-monthly magazine), Publications International Ltd, 1333 Grandview Parkway, Sturtevant, WI 53177
- o *Mary Beth's Bean Bag World Monthly*, H&S Media Inc, 2121 Waukegan Rd, Suite 120, Bannockburn, IL 60015
- o *Teddy Bear Guide Book* (annual publication), Barbie Hampton, editor, 15172 Koyle Cemetery Rd, Winslow, AR 72959 1-800-655-BEAR
- o *Teddy Bear and friends* (bi-monthly magazine), Cowles Enthusiast Media, 6405 Flank Dr, Harrisburg, PA 17112
- o *Teddy Bear Review* (bi-monthly magazine), Collector Communications Corp, 170 Fifth Ave, New York, NY 10010

Bear Events

- o Each August - Brookfield Zoo, Chicago, Illinois - Teddy Bear Picnic

o Each October -Teddy Bear Museum of Naples, Florida - Teddy Bear Picnic

Other

o Friends of Smokey Bear Balloon, 5912 Jones Place NW, Albuquerque, NM 87120 (nonprofit corporation of volunteers organized to develop and maintain a program of public education.)

o Good Bears of the World, PO Box 13097, Toledo, OH 43613

o The Hugging Bear Inn & Shoppe, Main St, Chester, VT 05143, 802/875-2412 (1850s Victorian mansion with tower and carriage house. A "bear in every bed" for guests to hug. Barn shop sells a diversity of bears. Inn hosts Vermont Teddybear Artists day in September each year.)

o Smokey Bear Campground, Hostel, Bed & Breakfast, Trans Canada Highway West, Revelstoke, British Columbia (13 rooms, 50 ft tall statue of Smokey)

o Dancing Bear Folk Center, 305 Buffalo Creek Secondary Rd, Thermopolis, WY 82443 (one wing of center is a teddy bear museum featuring Smokey and artist bears from around the world)

o Smokey Bear Museum, Smokey Bear Road (Hwy 380), Capitan, NM 88316-0730 (Smokey memorabilia, gift shop) Adjacent to the museum is Smokey Bear Historical State Park, garden burial place of Smokey I.

o Smokey Bear Historical State Park, 118 First Street, Capitan, MN 88316

o Teddy Bear Museum of Naples, 2511 Pine Ridge Rd, Naples, FL, 33941 Founded in 1990, the museum has over 3,000 bears. (Museum Director George B. Black, Jr. is an expert witness in court cases involving advertising bears.)

o Richard C. Yokley, Box 718, Bonita, CA 91908-0718 (Smokey Bear collector/researcher, will answer questions or share information.) E-mail: JYOKLEY@CTS.COM

For More Information

To find out more about the advertising bears covered in this book, consult the following books and articles.

Chapter 1: Smokey Bear

"Animal Attractions," *Remember* magazine, Aug/Sept 1994, pg. 6-7

Bergoffen, Bill, *100 Years of Federal Forestry, 1876-1976*, © 1977

Cain, Dean, *Film & TV Animal Star Collectibles*, Antique Trader Books, Dubuque, IA (Smokey memorabilia with price guide)

Davis, Kerra, "Those Illusive Ideal Bears," *Teddy Bear and friends*, Mar/April 1993, pg. 84-86

Dengler, Sandy, *Smokey, A Simple Country Bear Who Made Good*, Northwest Interpretive Association, 1987

Lawter, William, Jr., *Smokey Bear 20252*, Lindsay Smith Pub., 1994

Michaud, Terry and Doris, "Smokey Bear's 50th Birthday," *Teddy Bear and Friends*, Jul/Aug 1994, pg. 80-83

Morrison, Ellen Earnhardt, *Guardian of the Forest, A History of the Smokey Bear Program*, Morielle Press, Alexandria, Virginia, 1976

Mullins, Linda, *American Teddy Bear Encyclopedia*, 1995, Chapter Six, pg. 119-128

"Raikes Smokey," *Teddy Bear and friends*, Jul/Aug 1994, pg. 94-97, 45

Rinehart, Joyce, "Happy 50th Smokey," *Collectibles Country and Americana,* Winter 1994, pg. 72-75

Schmid, Jeanette, "Smokey Bear in the Air," *Teddy Bear and friends*, Jan/Feb 1995, p 85-86

USDA, Forest Service, *Smokey Bear's Story of the Forest*, illustrated by Harry Rossoll, (initial release 1951, with several subsequent printings, including 1979)

USDA, Forest Service, *The True Story of Smokey the Bear*, 1959 (comic book format) (other copyright dates 1960, 1964, and 1969, reprinted almost annually including 1991)

Chapter 2: Storybook Spokesbears

Berenstain Bears

Lawlor, Julia, "Kids' New Heroes," *USA Weekend*, Oct 4-6, 1996, pg. 20-21

Care Bears

Lindenberger, Jan, *Care Bear Collectibles,* Schiffer Publishing, 1997

Paddington Bear

Hockenberry, Dee, *More Enchanting Friends: Storybook Characters, Toys, and Keepsakes*, Schiffer, (Paddington, Pooh, Punkinhead, etc.)

Kinsey, Michilinda, "Happy Bearthday, Paddington!", *Teddy Bear and friends*, Jan/Feb 1998, pg. 52-53, 70

Rush, Pat, "40 Years With Paddington," *Teddy Bear Review*, Nov/Dec 1998, pg. 118-119

Wilson, Jacqueline, "The Many Charms of Paddington Bear," *Doll Designs*, Apr/May 1992, pg. 14-16

Yogi Bear

Porter, Margo Vanover, "Tracking Down a Smarter-Than-the-Average Bear," *Beans & Bears!* magazine, August 1999, pg. 117-118

Winnie the Pooh

"Disney Winnie the Pooh Stamps Incite Collector Stampede!" *USA Weekend*, Dec 12-14, 1997, pg. 24

Hockenberry, Dee, *Enchanting Friends: Collectible Poohs, Raggedies, Golliwogs and Roosevelt Bears*, 1995, Schiffer

Smith, Carol J. *Identification & Price Guide for Winnie the Pooh Collectibles, I*,

Smith, Carol J. *ID & Price Guide to Winnie the Pooh Collectibles, II*

Smith, Carol J., "The Perennial Appeal of Pooh Puppets," *Teddy Bear Review*, Jul/Aug 1998, pg. 65-67

Chapter 3: Baseball Bears

"Cooperstown Ball Park Bears," *Teddy Bear and friends*, Nov-Dec 1994, pg. 86- 87

Chapter 4: Other Beary Good Sports

Colby, Robert E., "The Lands' End Bears," *Teddy Bear Review*, Jan/Feb 99, pg. 69-71

Reed, Robert, "Sports-Event Dolls Worth Cheering About," *Doll World*, Apr 1998, pg. 14-15

Sarno, John, "This is Cooperstown, Too?!" *Teddy Bear Review*, Jul/Aug 1998, pg. 68-71

Chapter 6: Medical Bears

"New Arrivals," (Sir Koff-A-Lot), *Teddy Bear and friends*, Feb 1994, pg. 22

Chapter 7: Bears That Educate

Bradlaw, June A., (niece of Harry Rossoll), *Tree Bear's Adventure in Learning*, illustrations by Harry Rossoll, awaiting publication.

Fazio, James R., "New Bear in the Woods," (Tree Bear) *National Woodlands*, Oct 1996, pg. 16-17

Chapter 9: Those Foreign Fellows

Hockenberry, Dee, "Teddy Bear Price Guide," (Merrythought Punkinhead), *Teddy Bear and friends*, Nov 1998, pg. 16

Rush, Pat, "Merrythought Memories," (Punkinhead), *Teddy Bear Review*, Mar/Apr 1999, pg. 82-84

Wilson, Jacqueline, "Teddy Bear Mascots," (Canadian) *Doll Designs*, Jan 1992, pg. 14-16

Wilson, Jacqueline, "Panda Power," (China), *Doll Designs*, Sept 1993, pg. 34-35

Wilson, Jacqueline, "Wild 'n' Wooly...The Teddies of China," *Doll World*, Feb 1993, pg. 56-58

General Advertising Bear Information

Crisp, Marty, *Teddy Bears in Advertising Art*, Hobby House Press, 1991

Hake, Ted, *Hake's Guide to Advertising Collectibles, 100 Years of Advertising from 100 Famous Companies*, Wallace-Homestead, 1992

Lampher, Mary Jane, *Zany Characters of the Ad World*, Collector Books, 1995

Reed, Robert, *Bears and Dolls in Advertising, A Guide to Collectible Characters and Critters*, Antique Trader Books, 1998

Rinehart, Joyce, "Huckster Bears," *Collectibles: Country and Americana*, Fall 1994, pg. 72-74

Robinson, Jolee Ashman & Kay F. Sellers, *Advertising Dolls, Identification and Value Guide*, Collector Books, 1980

Sabo, Sandra R., "Bear Crazy," *Beans & Bears*, June 1999, pg. 56-57

MORE SCHIFFER TITLES

www.schifferbooks.com

The Bear Made Me Buy It: Product Advertising Bears. Joyce Gerardi Rinehart. For bear lovers and advertising buffs alike, collectors and non-collectors, this book is a must; it is destined to become "the" definitive reference work on bears that advertise products. With more than 500 previously unpublished color photographs, this first-of-its-kind book spotlights bears used to entice us to purchase products. More than three dozen collectors have shared their bear treasures of great diversity, from expensive limited editions to easily affordable bears found hibernating at flea markets and thrift shops. The bears advertise readily recognized trademarked products and appear on signage and packaging, as well as "bearly" edible foods and "other beary good stuff." This comprehensive look into the what, where, and how of advertising bears is sure to include your favorites.

Size: 8 1/2" x 11" 862 color photos 160 pp.
Price Guide
ISBN: 0-7643-0734-7 soft cover $29.95

Wonderful Raggedy Anns. Joyce Gerardi Rinehart. Color photographs depict previously unpublished dolls and related items. For the first time, creative "concept Raggedys" are covered in depth, and Raggedys dressed for the holidays also make their appearance. Volland, Georgene, Knickerbocker, and Applause collectors will welcome the sections provided to help them date their dolls.

Size: 8 1/2" x 11" 729 color photos 200 pp.
Price Guide
ISBN: 0-7643-0277-9 soft cover $29.95

Bear Sightings in Everyday Life. Dee Hockenberry. Over 475 color photographs show images of toy and real bears on everyday objects, and each is dated and identified with historical facts and a current value range. Old and new images of bears appear as useful and decoratve items; in metals, wood, glass, ceramics, paper, and textiles; from advertising and postage stamps to clothing and tablewares.

Size: 8 1/2" x 11" 483 color photos 160 pp.
Price Guide
ISBN: 0-7643-0872-6 hard cover $34.95

Enchanting Friends: Collectible Poohs, Raggedies, Golliwoggs, & Roosevelt Bears. Dee Hockenberry. These loveable toys have inspired related books, art works, beloved stuffed toys, licensed products and interpretations for several generations–highlighted in this delightful collectors' guide. Color photographs show the tremendous variety of material that can be found relating to these characters.

Size 8 1/2" x 11" 625 color photos 160 pp.
Price Guide
ISBN: 0-88740-723-4 hard cover $29.95